Archive Buildings
in the
United Kingdom
1993-2005

Archive Buildings
in the
United Kingdom
1993-2005

Christopher Kitching

Phillimore

2007

Published by
PHILLIMORE & CO. LTD
Shopwyke Manor Barn, Chichester, West Sussex, England
www.phillimore.co.uk

ISBN 978-1-86077-443-0

Printed and bound in Great Britain

CONTENTS

Preface and acknowledgements   vii

PART ONE

Introduction   1

Planning

1   Archives and archive buildings: the nature of the challenge   5
2   Functions: linkage and segregation   13
     Appendix: Headings towards a brief for an archive building   26
3   The site   27

Building

4   Structure and materials   31
     (i) General considerations   31
     (ii) Overall shape   39
     (iii) Individual structural features   41
     Appendix: Commissioned works of art   45
5   Security   47
6   Fire prevention   52
7   Environmental control   58
8   Conversion of existing buildings   67

Conclusion   74

PART TWO

Case Studies   75
Archive building projects in the UK completed 1993-2005   139

Notes   140
Bibliography   143
Synopsis of subjects in Part One   147

PREFACE AND ACKNOWLEDGEMENTS

The groundwork for this book was laid while I was employed by The National Archives (TNA) although most of the work was carried out shortly after my retirement, with the help of a generous travel grant from the Society of Archivists Research Fund which ensured that I could visit as many as possible of the archive buildings newly built, converted or extended in this period. The two bodies together have sponsored publication of the results. I am most grateful to them, and especially to Elizabeth Hallam Smith and Chris Woods, for their support and encouragement for and during the project.

Among many colleagues who provided advice and guidance at an early stage, not least by assisting me to identify the buildings to be studied, special thanks are due to Peter Anderson, Mary Ellis, Bruce Jackson, Norman James, Katie Norgrove, Louise Ray and Liz Rees, and to everyone in TNA's National Advisory Services. Peter Wojtyczka provided technical assistance at an early stage of the project, and Leah Chapman and Esmerelda O'Hagan administrative support.

The smooth course of the research depended critically on the patience and cooperation of the archivists in charge of all the buildings, especially of the 75 that I was able to visit in the course of the survey. Their kindness in showing me round, answering my many questions, and in some cases supplying plans and photographs to assist the study, made it a wholly pleasurable task. My thanks not only to them but also to their architects and governing bodies for their assistance.

Part One of the text was read in draft by Hugh Edgar, Helen Forde, Tim Harris, Norman James, Nick Kingsley, Ruth Kitching and Ian Milford. I am most grateful to them all for their expert comments which have helped me to make significant revisions and clarifications. The Case Studies in Part Two were each agreed in draft with the respective repositories. I am responsible for the simplified sketch plans appended to the case studies, but they are based on original architects' drawings which I gratefully acknowledge. I am also responsible for the photographs (but not for the weather conditions in which they were taken), except where a separate acknowledgement is given in the text.

A *terminus ad quem* had to be set, otherwise the work could have continued indefinitely. I decided on a rather arbitrary (and self-denying) basis that no building that had not been opened to the public by the end of 2005 would be included in this study, even though this leaves out a number of important examples that are nearing completion. When it came to the selection of case studies an even more difficult challenge had to be faced, since many more than the thirty featured in the previous book were of a standard worth considering this time round. I have stretched the number very marginally, selecting for inclusion those examples that seemed to have most to contribute to our understanding of the genre. The choice will not satisfy everyone, but after all, the chef is privileged to choose the ingredients of the feast!

Christopher Kitching
March 2006

PART ONE

INTRODUCTION

Scope of the volume

This is a sequel to *Archive buildings in the United Kingdom 1977-1992* (HMSO, 1993), which is now out of print. It is not exactly a 'second edition', because whilst much of the text of the first part of that book is incorporated here, it has been completely revised and re-ordered, and all of the case studies, as well as most of the incidental references, relate to a whole new generation of buildings. There are also a number of new features, including more emphasis on problems that have actually arisen during the period, with hints or recommendations on how to avoid them. As with the previous book, it is hoped that this volume will appeal to archivists and librarians in training, to the growing number of architects and engineers faced with designing a new archive building, and to all those involved in planning this process or who have a wider interest in archives and the heritage.

As before, the primary focus of the book is on providing all-round protection to the archives, and thus on the role of the building itself as the foundation for any Preservation Strategy. Less attention is paid to details of furniture and equipment, and to functions other than archive storage, than might perhaps have been desirable if the whole story were to be told. But this is largely because others have covered that ground, occasionally in very large books, and their work is in no need of duplication. Pointers are given to additional reading throughout the text, and a Bibliography is also supplied for those who would like to take their study further.

So what's new, 1993-2005?
Investment

The period under review, 1993-2005, has seen a remarkable flowering of archive buildings in the United Kingdom. Well over one hundred buildings have been taken into account in this survey, and 75 of them have been visited. They include those newly built, extended or converted for the first time to archival use in this period.

Astonishingly for such a small sector, these together represent an estimated capital layout of a quarter of a billion pounds (£250m).[1]

This scale of investment has been made possible first of all by the conscientious commitment of funds towards the care of their archives by governing bodies of our many archive services, at national and university level, in local government and business, and in many smaller organisations ranging from cathedrals to schools and charities.[2]

Many of these developments, however, would have been impossible had the down-payments of the governing bodies not attracted the generous multiplier effect of grants from the Heritage Lottery Fund (HLF), whose intervention, although not easily quantified overall for a variety of reasons, has been perhaps the most significant influence on the sector in this period. Other sources of financial support have included European Regional Development grants, the regional development agencies in the UK, local and national trusts sponsoring particular projects or such objectives as works of art within a building, and, particularly in the national and university sectors, a number of individual and corporate benefactors. Sometimes archive services have been fortunate enough to attract the support of multiple benefactors. In the case of Denbighshire Record Office for example, these included (as well as the county council) the HLF, CADW, the Welsh Tourist Board and the Welsh Development Agency. In the university sector, a series of funding initiatives from Non-formula Funding to the Research Libraries Support Programme provided additional cash, some of which went towards archive buildings.

New partnerships

Partnerships of many different kinds have had an impact on the provision of archive buildings and services during the period, bringing in new funding streams and/or new methods of working and perhaps economies of scale. Sometimes an archive service has been provided in association with one or more other services of the same parent authority, particularly local studies libraries or museum services (as at Bury, Greenwich, Perth, Rochdale, Surrey and elsewhere), but also including tourist offices and archaeology units; family history societies and the Victoria County History (Essex); and even a talking newspaper and a biodiversity centre (Orkney). Sometimes two adjacent local authorities, like Chester City and Cheshire county and many new unitary authorities working with the county from which they were detached (*see below*), have worked together to provide a single archive service. It is less easy to straddle the divide between one kind of funding body and another, but such arrangements are not unknown: take, for instance, those between a local authority and a university, as in Norfolk (other examples are actively under discussion); a local authority and a national body (Devon and the National Meteorological Archive), or a university and a business (Warwick and BP).

Statutory, regulatory and infra-structural changes

Many other changes have come about in this period in the environment in which archive services operate, and many of these too have helped to promote awareness of the need for archives and for new and improved archive buildings. Some of them were statutory, starting with the Local Government Acts of 1994 to 1996 which reorganised local authorities in England, Wales and Scotland and created many new unitary authorities which then had to make some arrangements for their archives. The Freedom of Information Act 2000 focused the attention of public authorities on the need to provide for their records and archives. The Disability Discrimination Act 1995 required many changes to be made to both existing and new public buildings to improve access.

Regulatory as well as statutory changes have also had an important influence. Most important for the purposes of this book was the publication in 2000 of a new edition of British Standard 5454, *Recommendations for the storage and exhibition of archive buildings*, about which I have written in more detail elsewhere.[3] Meanwhile on the international plane a new International Standard (ISO 11799) covered much the same ground, although in more general terms. The coming

together of the Public Record Office and the Historical Manuscripts Commission in 2003 to form The National Archives (TNA), led to the formulation of a Framework of Standards to embrace all other relevant standards in the field of archives, and a revision of the *Standard for record repositories*.[4]

Other important infra-structural changes have included the creation, in England, of MLA (the council for Museums, Libraries and Archives) and its regional agencies and in Wales, CyMAL. Advocacy for archives, by these bodies but also by the National Council on Archives,[5] the Archives Task Force[6] and others has been another important catalyst in the development of archive services.

Technical advances

This has also been a period of important technical advances, first of all in computer applications affecting every aspect of archive service delivery but in particular introducing the possibility of digitisation of images and, as a result, online access not only to catalogues (for which whole new programmes and partnerships including Access to Archives[7] have been developed) but also images of original documents. This has radically changed the nature of demand for, and indeed the very *locus* of, archive services. Computerised access to catalogues has resulted in the provision of separate rooms for this service, and/or terminals on readers' desks. The onward march of digitisation has resulted in the need for new technical services and the space in which to house them, and wireless networking, in its turn, is beginning to affect the layout of search rooms and other spaces to which the public have access. Increasingly, archive services are having to cope with archival and record material that is 'born digital'; this is giving rise to much new research and to new partnerships for effective preservation. Whilst it is clear that provision for digital materials will be an increasingly important aspect of archive services in the future, it is not yet clear what the impact will be on archive buildings.

Among other technical advances could be cited the development of aspirating fire detection systems which detect a fire in the incipient phase.[8] The need to replace halon as a fire-suppressing agent under the terms of the Montreal Protocol, has led to the development of improved water-based applications as well as new gases for use in fire suppression. These are considered in the appropriate chapter below.

Research and development

Research into the possibilities of natural climatisation of buildings – that is to say the control of ventilation, temperature and relative humidity without recourse to air-conditioning, and with as little mechanical intervention as possible – has also continued apace. Not only have important results been published, but a number of serious attempts have been made to apply the research in practice, beginning with Jersey Archive[9]. There have been rather mixed degrees of success when using this approach, but since many air-conditioned repositories have no less difficulty in meeting BS 5454's recommendations with regard to the storage environment there is every incentive for this research and development to continue, one hopes with improved success rates and/or with more specific guidance as to the amount of mechanical back-up that is necessary to make an otherwise naturally-climatised building function well (*see chapter 7*).

This is one of the biggest issues still unresolved in this field. But it is not the only one where important research has contributed to our understanding of buildings and how they can serve the needs of archives: progress has been made, for example, in pollution control, thanks to the work of the Centre for Sustainable Heritage at University College London (established within the period under review);[10] and in such matters as the moisture-absorbing properties of building materials.[11]

There is much more to be learnt from international research and practice in this period. The Committee on Archive Buildings in Temperate Climates (CBTE) of the International Council on Archives has now been disbanded but the fruits of its work have mostly been published either in the ICA journal *Janus* or on the ICA website, which includes an important bibliography compiled by Arnold den Teuling and revised by Ted Ling.[12] The Centro de Información Documental de Archivos in Madrid, through its regular *Boletín* and its website,[13] has also made a significant contribution to the bibliography of this and other archival subjects. The systematic research of the Archive Centre for Professional and Technical Problems, Maribor, Slovenia, has for the most part been published in its journal *Atlanti*. Important books about the archive buildings of a number of individual countries have also been published, including Ted Ling's *Solid, safe, secure: building archive repositories in Australia* (1998) and, from the Direction des Archives de France, *Les bâtiments d'archives 1986/2003* (2004).

Library and museum buildings in this period also offer important parallels, and much has been done both in the UK and elsewhere to disseminate good practice in these domains.[14]

Changing patterns of use

The growing popularity of family and local history, and the greatly increased attention to archives by radio and television, have contributed to a steady increase in reader visits to archive services throughout this period. At the same time, the ready availability online of archive catalogues, and of digitised images of original documents, has led to a surge in demand for remote, electronic access. Both these trends have had an effect on the design and fitting out of archive buildings, and some entire buildings, such as the Family Records Centre in Islington (run jointly by the General Register Office and TNA) and the Worcestershire Family History Centre in Worcester, have been dedicated to this specific kind of demand.

Other factors

The 'snowball effect' should not be ignored. The more archive buildings of a high standard there are to compare, the easier it is to judge what one might need when planning a new one. And the harder it is to put up with something less than the best! Across the archive profession, real encouragement has been drawn from the recently developed buildings and from the generosity of their custodians in showing aspirants round and answering practical questions.

On a more sombre note, the Norwich fire of 1994 and the widespread floods of 2000-2001, some of which affected archives, coupled with growing evidence of global warming and the risk of rising sea levels, have all served to focus minds on why archives need to be protected even more systematically than in the past.

Overall impressions

The United Kingdom has now much to be proud of in the building-stock for its archives, and this book includes some strikingly attractive new buildings and some successful and interesting conversions, as well as many plainer but no less functional examples. The progress that has been achieved in these years, given the small scale of the archive domain, has been truly remarkable, although there remain some less fortunate authorities that have not yet had their opportunity. It is hoped that they will draw encouragement from what others have achieved.

Chapter 1

ARCHIVES AND ARCHIVE BUILDINGS: THE NATURE OF THE CHALLENGE

Growing pains

Archives accumulate unrelentingly. As a general rule there is not the kind of turnover of stock[1] associated with say a lending library or a commercial warehouse, but rather the continual addition of new items or whole new collections which, like those already held, are intended for permanent preservation. This is true whether by 'archives' we mean simply the historic administrative records of the parent organisation or, as the term is more commonly applied by public repositories, the whole range of material acquired by transfer, gift, purchase, loan or statutory deposit.[2]

Predicting their accrual rate however is notoriously difficult. To date there has been no appreciable reduction in the flow of paper documents into archives as a result of the increase in electronic documentation. The 'paperless office' may well prove illusory. The annual *increase* in the amount of physical space required for archive storage, as opposed to cyber space, might well decline significantly in future but, irrespective of any such trend, for the next generation and more there are many years' worth of paper archives still to be transferred.

Annual averages of accessions may be useful for forward planning but they can so easily be overtaken by unforeseen events. For example, legislation has repeatedly directed or encouraged the transfer to public repositories of large quantities of records which were previously held elsewhere. In some instances, registration records of births, marriages and deaths previously held by local registrars have recently passed to local record offices. The closure of hospitals and restructuring in health services has similarly contributed to major transfers of archives at short notice. The Freedom of Information Act 2000 has encouraged public authorities to take additional steps for the care of their records and archives and to transfer more into official custody. Business mergers, and business failures, have resulted in large quantities of archives on the move. Hardly had Diageo provided a new store for its archives, at Menstrie in Stirlingshire, when it had also to take in the Guinness archives from Park Royal, which it could only do by extending the building. On another front altogether, unrepeatable opportunities have arisen quite unexpectedly to acquire large collections of family or business papers by bequest or private treaty sale or at auction. It is also widely reported that the very existence of a new building, with all the publicity attached to it, encourages owners of archives to seek to transfer them into safe keeping. The first two years of the new Norfolk Archive Centre saw accessions at double the average rate.

So space planned to last for many years can fill up much more quickly than expected. Provision for regular growth, but also with a small extra margin for unforeseen accruals, ought therefore to be a normal commitment on the part of those authorities which offer a public archive service. Regrettably this has often been overlooked or pushed aside by budgetary constraints.

Amid all the competing claims on public funds, archive services have tended to be given low priority. Some of the services whose new premises are celebrated in this volume had long been overdue for a move from almost unmanageable circumstances, with records scattered in accommodation inadequate by today's standards, including out-stores remote from the main building and of inferior quality. Without exception, whatever the continuing problems with the new premises, the improvement compared with the previous arrangements for custody and access has been striking. After the great growth and renewal of the sector over the past thirty years, and especially in the period under review, the proportion of archive services in the direst straits has been significantly reduced. Sadly, however, there are still too many exceptions to the general success story.

Additional, or alternative, accommodation?

Once an authority accepts that additional or alternative accommodation is required for its archives, and commits the necessary capital, it has several options, not all of which require the purchase or construction of a new building, most notably:

- to place little-used, or unused, archives in commercial storage or with another archive service that has spare storage capacity at least in the short term;

- in the case of an archive within a larger organisation, to colonise and convert additional parts of the existing building (referred to below as *in situ* conversion);

- to acquire or build one or more out-stores, while retaining the original building;

- to extend on-site where space permits;

- to commission a new, purpose-built repository to hold everything;

- to acquire an alternative building for conversion.

Other permutations are possible, for example:

- to acquire one building for conversion but to purpose-build another one alongside it (Diageo, English Heritage National Monuments Record, Leicestershire);

- to acquire an existing building to use as a shell or frame, whilst in effect purpose-building a free-standing repository inside it (Barclays Group, Devon, Gloucestershire, Oxfordshire);

- to acquire a building on a short-term basis pending the development of a longer-term solution (Guardian/Observer, University College London);

- to retain an existing building but provide in addition a second (or third) building to accommodate just some of the functions (as at the National Archives of Scotland, Thomas Thomson House which has no public services).

Fig.1 gives a broad indication of the choices made during this period.

The choice is not always clear-cut, nor is it always taken with full thought for the consequences. For example, good quality out-stores may be a practical and cost-effective solution, especially if reserved mainly for those records which are least in demand. But there has been a marked tendency among the authorities providing archive services to suppose that such auxiliary buildings can somehow make do with second-rate standards of custody, particularly with regard to security and environmental controls. This is a fallacy. The recommendations of BS 5454 should be seen as applying equally to all materials that are intended to be preserved permanently, and to all premises in which they are housed.

Consideration of the case for and against conversion is deliberately deferred until a later chapter, because before looking for solutions we need to know our specifications. To what standards should the building conform? What functions and services must it accommodate both now and in the future? How long is that future to be: 5, 10, 15, 20 years or more? And is there an obvious strategy beyond that? With answers to those kinds of questions, real

	national	HE	local	business	other specialist	total
New build	5 Incl Jersey	16	14	1	6	42
Conversion plus new build	1	2	4	1	1	9
First time conversion	-	4	16	5	3	28
Conversion in existing premises	3	8	8	3	7	29
Total	9	30	42	10	17	108

Fig. 1 *Archive building projects in the UK completed 1993-2005*

planning and the search for a site or building can begin.

Timescales

(a) the expected/planned life of a new building

BS 5454 (s.4.2) recommends a minimum planned life of 15 to 20 years for an archive building. This is *not* of course the period for which the building's structure and fabric will survive (which should be appreciably longer and might even be measured in centuries), but rather the period until that building is expected to be full and unable to take any more archives, after which other solutions will need to be developed. If the planned life is too short, the planning and upheaval will have to be undertaken again uncomfortably soon; if too long, there is a risk of costly accommodation lying idle. In general, in this period storage capacity has been planned to last for between 10 and 25 years depending on the commissioning authority's circumstances and the availability of alternative properties, or of adjacent space, for extension or modular development.

On the other hand it is sometimes forgotten that other functions besides storage may expand or contract over a 10- to 20-year period. Allowance has to be made for any foreseeable increases or decreases in staff (including contract staff working on short-term projects), readership and other public (eg educational) visits, and for changes in technology requiring, for example, additional microfilm readers or computer terminals, and associated cabling.

The best laid plans can be frustrated, not only by the arrival of records in bulk from an unexpected source as hinted at above, but also by changes to the proposed building on the insistence of the planning authority. For example, the height of the National Archives of Scotland's Thomas Thomson House was restricted lest it interfere with the radar for aircraft approaching Edinburgh airport.

(b) the run-in time for a new building

A considerable time can elapse between an authority's being committed in principle to a new building or extension and the day of its eventual occupation. There have been many false starts, for example where a particular site or building under investigation proved unobtainable, unsuitable or unaffordable.

Indeed it is not uncommon for a single project to have several successive disappointments of this kind. Where a new building is required it will be prudent, at least in the case of public sector archive services, to allow a minimum of five years as the run-in time, to take account of political, financial and planning considerations as well as site acquisition, tendering and building. In some cases it has taken considerably longer.

Planning can be a lengthy and professionally demanding process. For archivists, the text-book approach[3] posits time for reflection, research, discussion and refinement, involving all the staff and other prominent stakeholders in the operation and clearing away mutual misconceptions between the funding body, the architect, the archivist and the contractors about the objectives of the exercise, the nature and style of the building, and the financial and other constraints. Typical stages on the way are illustrated in Fig. 2.[4] In practice, circumstances may demand improvisations, refinements and short-cuts, or additional or repeated stages, and some stages such as the identification of a site may come earlier or later than indicated.[5] In the public sector, for example, depending on the value of the contract(s), a further delay may arise from the need to advertise the tender through the Official Journal of the European Community.

For a building of the scale and national importance of the British Library at St Pancras or the second building of the PRO (now The National Archives) at Kew, planning of course involved a team of experts over a long period, and time to take wide soundings of the needs of readers and of the neighbouring community. In the British Library's case some twenty years elapsed from first plans to completion, and in the meantime many changes had come about including the absorption of the India Office Records, so that adaptations and compromises were necessary along the way. In Devon's case, the process took about seven years, allowing for tying up all the partnerships for occupancy of this shared-use building, not to mention funding partnerships. A similar run-in time was experienced at Girton College Cambridge. For smaller repositories the time available for preparing and presenting the case, drafting and revising the plans and seeing the project through has been very varied, but some have proceeded with remarkable speed and economy.

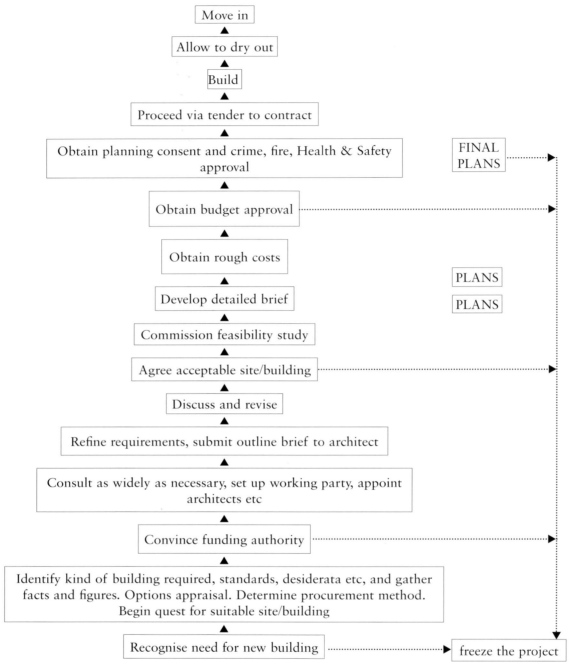

Fig. 2 *Summary of planning stages*

The Leonard Cheshire Archive building took 16 months to plan and only 16 weeks to build.[6] The time-scale is not always of one's own choosing but may be driven by external events. For example at the Royal Academy of Arts the opportunity to plan a new archive facility came unexpectedly, as a by-product of the wider development plan for the Fine Rooms: the archivist had to mobilise his forces rapidly to devise a brief and seize the moment.

Plans which have lain unexecuted for a number of years will almost certainly need review to take account of the most recent developments in design, materials and technology. Uncertainties over the future development of a service can result in a kind of planning blight, with the funding authority hesitant to commit resources to the refurbishment, or even the maintenance, of the premises until longer-term strategy has been resolved.

Procurement routes[7]

The method of procurement (and the form of contract) chosen will often be determined or constrained by the overall policy of the governing body, and/or by the requirements of any partner organisations or of a particular scheme under which the project is to be financed. Essentially there will be a choice between 'traditional procurement' where design and construction are handled by different individuals or organisations, 'design and build', where a single contractor undertakes both design and construction, 'construction management' where one contractor manages the build but the construction work is put out to separate tender, and 'design, build, finance and operate' (as in a Private Finance Initiative scheme).[8] Other scenarios are possible.

Likely cost

It is difficult to determine the final costs until quite late in the planning process, when detailed specifications have been drawn up for building, plant, equipment and furniture, but for budgetary purposes some estimate has to be made. Fig.3 gives some examples of recent costs. When it comes to the detail (the headings and nature of individual costs that need to be taken into account) the cost model developed for libraries by Leighton and Weber[9] is highly relevant to archives also. Comparisons are precarious because of differing costing practices and differences in the standards aimed at. Some, for example, have built on land they already owned, others have first had to buy the site. This is not apparent in the figures. Similarly, some have benefited from being able to sell off or return to their parent authority the premises or site they already occupied, the resulting savings being put towards the budget.

Whole Life Costing[10]

BS 5454:2000 (s.5.1.3) recommends Whole Life Costing, that is, costing extrapolated/ discounted throughout the building's entire projected life (of say 20-25 years). On this basis, heavy initial capital costs – for example to achieve high thermal inertia in the fabric

and thereby minimise mechanical intervention, or to use best quality durable materials and finishes throughout and thereby cut down the frequency of redecoration or replacements (as was done in the British Library) – can be seen in a much more favourable light than might at first appear. It has been estimated that £10,000 put into research on the means of delivering passive environmental control at Jersey Archives led to a saving of £300,000 in capital outlay.[11] The cost of the stainless steel roof of Thomas Thomson House (National Archives of Scotland) could be offset against its low predicted maintenance costs. Conversely, any accruing costs of energy-intensive machinery, or regular replacement costs for ICT or other equipment, might in the long term prove a serious drain on resources, and the immediate benefits of a Public Finance Initiative scheme might be seen in a different light in terms of both cost and flexibility in the longer term.

In practice, budgetary ceilings have often been imposed that prove unrealistically low in relation to the task in hand. Agonising, but absolutely necessary, decisions then have to be taken. For large-scale projects this might call for an exercise such as 'value engineering', as was done for Essex Record Office. This brings together not only the project planning team (archivists and professional staff, architect, engineer, quantity surveyor and so on) but also other stakeholders including the funding body, and a number of outside experts or assessors, preferably with an independent and practised facilitator, to apply as many brains as possible to the dilemma.

Where there is a budget shortfall, unless contingency or alternative funds may be drawn on or the load spread across several financial years, something has to be forgone or the whole project abandoned. Discounting any strategic over-bidding for funding and facilities, the governing body has to judge at what level of cutback the central objective of the scheme is compromised. Some have had to settle for a smaller building than originally planned, or for a lesser degree of environmental control or fire protection, to pare down requirements for secondary storage and staff accommodation, or to phase a conversion or the purchase of machinery and equipment over a number of years. The authorities responsible for caring for archives need to be aware of the scale of the commitment into which they are entering if they are to make adequate provision to meet their obligations.

What is an archive building like?

Archive building projects, although impressively numerous in this period, are still relatively rare in comparison with, say, libraries or museums. As a result only a few architects have specific expertise in archive buildings: for most, an archive building may be something they encounter only once in their career. Nor is the literature about archive buildings very extensive: architects' reference shelves are not overflowing with guides to their construction and layout, as they might be for libraries. To make matters worse, outside the national repositories archivists have on the whole been slow to describe their buildings in print, and there is no Central Direction of Archives to do it for them, as there is for example in France.[12] To some extent the present volume is designed to fill that gap, but more individual studies would be welcome.

For all this, the territory is by no means uncharted. BS 5454 is the first essential point of reference, and there is no shortage of published guidance on planning and briefing specifically for archive buildings, as well as useful comparative material on libraries.[13] Other sources of guidance that have been influential in the design of several buildings described in this volume are the unpublished briefs held by colleagues who have recently gone through a similar exercise, and of course visits to other buildings to see how the vision was turned into reality.

Whilst some archive buildings might be said to form 'families' of style, for example those with steeply overhanging roofs to carry rainwater clear of the walls and shelter them from the sun, the chief conclusion of this survey is that there is no single blueprint for success but rather a significant variety of acceptable approaches. The distinctive architectural character of many of the buildings studied shines through, and is a matter for celebration. And, to a greater extent than in the previous period, buildings of real architectural interest are strongly represented. Perhaps the lack of a universal solution is a good thing, as the differences between the needs and circumstances of any two authorities commissioning archive buildings can be as significant as the similarities.

The fundamental objectives

There are, however, two fundamental keys to success: and they are more a matter of objectives than of bricks and mortar. Every aspect of an archive building must, in this order, serve (1) to protect the archives against all forces which might otherwise harm them: in particular fire and water, physical or chemical change resulting from a polluted or under-regulated environment; dust, mould and vermin; theft and vandalism; and (2) to promote the work and well-being of everyone (staff and public alike) going about their business there.

An archive building is in a number of important respects *sui generis* precisely because archives themselves are unique and irreplaceable. Therefore it cannot be planned and built as though it were really something else (a library or warehouse, for example). If the chosen course is to convert an existing building (which really *was* something else), the question to be asked at the outset is whether it can match up to its required new character as an archive building.

The brief for a new building

Depending on the speed with which a project must be seen through, and the working preferences of individual architects, it can be necessary to proceed through several separate stages of briefing, beginning with no more than an outline and working towards a definitive document or documents which will guide the architect, engineers, surveyors and contractors through every phase. It is advisable for archivist and architect to have at least a preliminary discussion of requirements before anything is committed to writing.

The most effective brief is one that combines clear direction with succinctness and is focused on the needs of the particular authority and service without lengthy diversions into the nature of archives, security, or other key concepts (although these should have been discussed).

The French *Manuel d'archivistique* observes that with a good brief the architect cannot help produce a good building, whilst the archivist who draws up a deficient brief deserves all that is coming.[14] Headings towards a brief are given in an appendix to the next chapter.

It has also been said that the main challenge to the architect lies in giving substance, form

£ million	Building	Year	HLF
58	TNA	1995	N
11.2	National Archives of Scotland	1995	N
10.5	Essex	1999	N
7.0	Surrey	1998	Y
	London Metropolitan University (Women's Library)	2002	Y
6.7	Norfolk	2003	Y
6.5	York University Borthwick Institute	2005	Y
5.7	East Riding Treasure House (in progress)	2006	Y
5.0	Devon	2005	Y
4.6	English Heritage National Monuments Record	1993	N
4.5	Berkshire	2000	N
4.0	Guardian/Observer	2002	N
3.86	London Metropolitan Archives extension	1993	N
3.5	Oxfordshire	2000	Y
3.0	Denbighshire	2002	Y
	Southampton University Library	2004	Y
	Westminster	1995	N
2.5	Cambridge: Girton College	2005	N
2.3	Warwickshire extension	2003	Y
2.2	Hereford Cathedral Library	1996	Y
	Tate Gallery	2002	N
2.0	Cambridge: Churchill Archive Centre	2002	N
	Warwick University/BP	1993	N
1.8	Shropshire	1995	N
1.6	Leicestershire	1993	N
1.2	Bury (Manchester)	2005	Y
	York Minster Library	1998	Y
1.0	BT	1997	N
	North West Film Archive	1996	Y
	Tameside	2005	Y
0.9	Cardinal Tomás Ó Fiaich Library	1999	Y
0.78	Northern Region Film and TV Archive	2004	N
0.7	Cumbria (Whitehaven)	1996	N
	Yorkshire Film Archive	2003	Y
	Unilever	2004	N
0.5	Manchester City	1996	N
	Royal Academy	2002	N

Fig. 3 *COST: some examples, in descending order.*
Excluding projects where the archive was part of a larger scheme eg for a library or museum, and not separately costed. The final column indicates whether or not a HLF grant was made towards the cost. (Conversions costing below £0.5 million are not listed).

and style without confusing the building's proper priorities[15] or engaging in bravado; and that 'form follows function'.[16]

The architect's drawings, like the briefs from which they take their inspiration as to layout, orientation and general shape, are refinable documents. The first drafts in particular are for critical study, not uncritical admiration. Either

at this stage or once they have been revised to take account of the archivist's initial comments, they may be referred to the respective National Archives for comment.[17] It is rare, although not unknown, to find whole functions omitted in error or completely unviable layouts proposed, but this consultative stage provides an opportunity to raise pertinent points with the architect and consider alternative layouts, for example to promote greater security or make the building more easily manageable. Whilst it is the job of the architect to give expression and character to the building, this must not be at the expense of its functionality, and from time to time the archivist has to stand firm against misunderstandings of the essential requirements, or against the architect's 'flights of fancy'.

Some real problems reported

Some of the problems encountered during the planning phase have already been alluded to above, but many others have been reported during this survey, including the following:

- Cuts in the budget resulting, in different places, in the omission of air-conditioning and automated fire-suppression systems; the paring down of non-archival storage space (eg for stationery, cleaning, conservation, exhibition, education); the sacrifice of entire functions such as lecture and meeting facilities, education, conservation; the provision of wholly inadequate space for staff offices.

- The lack of provision within a large budget for viring between sub-heads, meaning that a small over-run on one subhead could not be offset against a saving elsewhere.

- The exclusion, or inadequate involvement, of professional staff from the archives in various stages of the planning process.

- Decisions made over the archivist's head without consultation, by well-meaning senior officers or other professionals eg engineers.

- Poor communication between the various parties (the parent authority and its senior managers, archivist, architect, etc).

- Provision made only for initial capital costs without sufficient thought for continuing running costs.

- Using an interested party, such as the architect, as project manager, which restricted full and frank discussion and failed to deliver proper scrutiny.[18]

- Changes in the structure or personnel of the parent authority during the project, resulting in loss of continuity of expertise and input.

- The architect believing that as archives were very old a conservative or antique style of building design would be most appropriate, when the commissioning authority was actually seeking a striking modern statement.

Recommendations

Some of the above problems may simply have to be lived with, but steps can be taken to minimise the likelihood or the impact of others.

In the public sector, it is usually mandatory, and elsewhere it may well be beneficial, to follow a specified project methodology.

- It is essential that the professional staff (archivist(s) and conservator(s)) be fully engaged and fully represented in the planning and design process.

- Every effort should be made to ensure that all involved are fully briefed as to what is required and why, and that good communications and regular face-to-face meetings are established at the outset to ensure that all are 'speaking the same language'.

- It may be beneficial to have a neutral chairman for the project committee.

- Taking decisions on the hoof, eg in response to time constraints during a project, can sometimes be unavoidable. When this happens it helps to have at least two people involved, especially if measurements or quantities need to be checked.

- Every stage must be clearly documented, for audit reasons but also in case there is a change of personnel during the project.

There is much more to be said in the next chapter about the planning and location of individual functions. This preliminary sketch has attempted merely to convey the essential nature of an archive building, and the issues which govern its very being.

Chapter 2

FUNCTIONS: LINKAGE AND SEGREGATION[1]

Preparing a checklist of functions

Before any new archive building can be planned, it is important to draw up a check-list of the various functions it should contain, and then to consider how these will be linked or segregated. The checklist will be invaluable as an *aide-mémoire* when it comes to drawing up the brief for the architect (see Appendix to this chapter).

For ease of reference, certain practical points about each function are considered here because they will need to be taken into account during the briefing process and the planning and execution of the project, although in practice some of these will arise at the building or fitting-out stages.

Some caveats

Needs will vary from one archive service to another, and so will opportunities, because some may not be able to find, or to afford to build premises large enough to accommodate all the functions they would ideally choose to include. Whilst this chapter draws widely on the experience of archives in this period, and so is not merely theoretical, the guidance it can offer can only be of a general nature. It will, for example, touch on certain functions which smaller services will not need to include in their checklist, and it may omit others which would be required in a more specialist repository such as a film or sound archive. So it should not be seen as offering an exact blueprint in any individual case.

Flexibility, now and in the future, also needs to be borne in mind. Planners must not delude themselves that patterns of occupancy and use will remain static and that every function on their list will have its own identifiable and fixed space for the building's full life. Many repositories in this period have run into unexpected and sometimes sudden changes of need for space. These have included:

- a shift in patterns of employment, resulting in more (or fewer) staff and volunteers having to be accommodated

- a shift in demand from microform to digital surrogates, resulting in different technical space requirements

- the acquisition of a major collection containing a large amount of oversize material or material in special media, affecting storage space requirements

- the suspension of whole functions, or the taking on of additional functions, as part of a wider strategy

- a sustained surge of public interest and visits following the opening of a new building.[2]

The storage areas apart, therefore, a degree of flexibility in the assignment of functions to particular rooms or spaces may well be desirable. This will need to be taken into account in the structure (consider, for example, the case for at least some de-mountable walls, sliding partitions) and in the provision of services such as power points and computer networking. Flexibility, as well as rigidity, however, comes at some cost and any benefits need to be teased out as part of the Whole Life Costing.

Segregation and linkage of functions

One question which has a bearing on every-thing else (from the choice of site/ground space required to the shape and layout of the build-ing/number of storeys, its structure and the materials employed) is the preferred approach to the linkage or segregation of functions.

Textbooks usually emphasise the desirability of segregating functions that demand different degrees of security, environmental control, fire prevention, human comfort, noise, and so on. But it is important not to become so obsessed with functional segregation as to miss the equally important inter-relationships which need to be achieved if risks and disturbance to archives and people are to be minimised.

The five main groups of functions tradition-ally found in an archive building are (1) storage, (2) plant, (3) offices, (4) technical services and (5) public areas, although further sub-division is possible, for example between storage for paper and parchment archives on the one hand and that for audio-visual and computer archives on the other, between wet and dry areas in conservation, or between relatively quiet and relatively noisy areas in the search room. Some degree of segregation is always to be found, and in the case of new buildings this is often apparent in their design and outward appearance.

Where to start?

The priority must lie with the **archive storage** areas, which should provide **secure custody in a stable and controlled environment**, as explained more fully in chapter 7. This may seem self-evident, but it often takes second place to the provision of an aesthetically pleasing building or state-of-the-art accommodation for front-line public services (which will help meet performance indicators), or to the convenient location of the archive service alongside related services; or else it is altogether scaled down for budgetary reasons. So it needs to be re-stated that without secure custody there is a risk of theft or damage to some or all of the holdings; and without a controlled environment the condition of the records may deteriorate until in extreme cases they become irreparable. In either event there would be a loss or diminution of the very resource upon which all the repository's other activities depend, so this really is the heart of the matter.

In positioning functions within the site plan, the main concern is to protect the storage area both horizontally and vertically from all risk of fire, water penetration, unauthorised intrusion, and threats to the stability of its internal

Plant room leak

environment. The first obvious candidates for segregation on these grounds are **plant rooms**, where leakage and condensation may be regular occurrences and where there might be real risks of fire or explosion.

But documents move around the building; they are not always safely tucked away in the strongroom. And danger may arise elsewhere: from machinery and equipment; from stores of chemicals or flammable materials; from water, drainage and sewerage services, rough handling, and so on. So segregation of the plant room alone is not a universal panacea and has to be backed up with careful management procedures and staff training.

Records, or at least the information they contain (which in order to reduce wear and tear on the originals may well be produced in a surrogate form such as microfilm or digitised images), are there to be consulted, otherwise they are not really objects 'of record' at all. But before consultation can happen they have to be sorted and described, and then both the records and the staff have to be managed. This requires **office and work space**. Experience unfortunately suggests that this tends to be skimped or to be among the first targets for savings when budgets have to be trimmed. And yet, where insufficient space is provided for these management functions staff morale can be sharply reduced and the efficiency of the whole operation threatened. Next to the records, the staff are the building's most important resource.

The care and management of archives calls in addition for **technical facilities** such as conservation, reprographics, computer services and processing facilities for specialist media such as film and sound archives. These are not always provided in-house but, where they are, they require planning of an order different from the main run of offices, with special attention to health and safety and to the provision of dedicated power, water and other services.

Many would regard **public access** as the principal *raison d'être* for an archive building. The public areas are certainly the most visible, and therefore most likely to attract comment in the wider world. So it is no accident that care and attention is everywhere being given to identifying and meeting users' needs, providing comfortable, accessible and well-appointed research facilities, conveniently linked to associated public amenities, and clearly demarcating them from areas of the building where, for their own good (health and safety) as well as that of the records (security, environmental control), the public should not venture. In this study, however, the care of the archives themselves claims prior attention.

At the planning stage two additional issues need to be addressed: namely **logistics** (getting people and documents efficiently from place to place around the building without passing unnecessarily through zones with different requirements as to security or environmental control) and **noise**. Much of the work undertaken in an archive building requires concentration. This can be assisted not only by strategically separating incompatible activities, but also by planning lines of communication to minimise the amount of to-ing and fro-ing and distraction and providing appropriately thick walls, and floor, ceiling and wall coverings that will absorb sound. Inter-connected rooms with no corridors to by-pass them promote excessive traffic. Noise inside the building can originate from: plant and machinery; lift doors and motors; vibrations carried along ducting, piping and wall surfaces; speech and laughter from enquiry desks, offices, lecture theatres, classrooms, staff rooms, kitchens and common rooms; keyboards and tape-recorders; radios and televisions used for educational purposes or (if allowed) in workshops; the slamming of doors and flushing of lavatories. Noise can also be generated from adjacent properties, or wholly from outside by traffic, aircraft, passers-by, building work or industrial activity, all of which should be taken into account when choosing the site.

Flow diagram

The checklist of functions can now be turned into a flow-diagram as in Fig. 4. It should be noted, however, that this is not a blue-print for the actual physical lay-out of the building, but only an indication of the relationships between functions. It is not based on any one building, and should not be used as a model without taking account of local conditions and preferences. Larger repositories devising such charts sometimes vary the thickness of the flow-lines to represent the relative volumes of traffic.

Translating this into a ground-plan, especially in a converted building, is the main challenge. Generally, the more spread-out the functions laterally or vertically, the more difficult the building is to manage economically and securely. And lines of communication, both horizontal and vertical, need special attention. What routes will (a) the records and (b) the people follow within the building? What mechanical assistance will be necessary (lifts, hoists, trolleys etc), and at what points? What obstacles (doors, stairs, corners etc) will be encountered in transit, and with what consequences for the building's security and environmental specifications and fire precautions? Will the largest document actually get through all the doors or corners on its routes? It is always useful to have an experienced independent eye cast over the plans before building commences.[3]

With these issues in mind we can now follow the various functions through the diagram, noting some of the practical points that have arisen in archive buildings of this period.[4]

Delivery/loading bay

A covered delivery bay, sadly omitted as an economy measure in a few instances, protects records from the elements. It needs to be covered by the intruder alarm system, especially if it is out of sight at the rear of the building, and for added security its door(s) should be openable only from the inside. Additional surveillance by closed-circuit TV, entry phones and security lighting is sometimes provided.

Where canopies or drive-in bays are used, their ceiling and any projections such as gutters have to allow for the highest vehicle expected and, if the land slopes, for the tilt of the vehicle. Vehicles and buildings alike have had unfortunate scrapes where this was overlooked. The doors of a loading bay should never open directly into the archival storage area, as this will affect the internal environment and may introduce pollution from vehicle exhausts. Instead, they should open only into a dedicated delivery/reception area which is itself outwith the main archival strongroom(s) even if, as is desirable, it has comparable security and environmental controls and fire rating.

Loading platforms of fixed heights have caused logistical problems, and a mechanical platform/hoist, a metal roller conveyor belt or a fork-lift truck may be desirable equipment.

Problems reported include:

- loading bay not accessible from the road in the final (as-built) layout
- inadequate turning space for vehicles
- loading bay opening directly into the archive store, with vehicles allowed to reverse in, as in a warehouse.

Archive reception room(s)/accessions suite

Reception

Adjacent to the delivery bay, or occasionally on another floor but connected to it by a goods lift, there is usually a reception room/area where the records may be given a preliminary health check, and any needing treatment for mould or insect infestation isolated (*see below*). In larger repositories (Berkshire, Devon, Norfolk) there is sometimes a suite of rooms, side by side or one off the other, for reception, isolation and accessioning. Storage space unimpeded by columns, heaters etc is a welcome asset here. Fittings such as shelves or pigeon-holes and tables vary with local preference. Where modern records management is offered by the same service, that may require its own reception room.

Drying/isolation

Fumigation rooms, which used to be thought essential, have been almost completely abandoned in UK archive repositories, both on health and safety grounds and also because more effective treatments have been developed.[5] Isolation and/or drying of any records infested with mould or pests can however still be necessary and a room or rooms are therefore often provided for this purpose, sometimes equipped with specialist freezers (to kill off insect infestations) or freeze-dryers (for the treatment of damp or wet archives). The drying/isolation area should have an independent air handling and/or extraction system in order to reduce the risk of mould and pests spreading to other parts of the building.

Sorting room(s)

Over and above the space allocated for initial reception and isolation, it is usual to provide a separate room or rooms for sorting. Sorting of any dirty archives cannot conveniently be undertaken in a general office, and sorting of large documents or bulky archives requires considerable table-top and possibly also trolley space. The experience of some repositories, however, is that dedicated sorting rooms located some distance from the main staff offices tend to be spurned by staff, and the work transferred elsewhere in the building in order to avoid a sense of isolation for staff working alone, so this is another factor that needs to be considered in placing the sorting room. At the minimum, dedicated sorting rooms should have telephone and computer connections with the rest of the building. Large movable trolleys, or even work benches on wheels (as at the British Library) allow the sorting space to be used more flexibly than do fixed work benches, although in many cases both will be necessary.

Archive strongrooms[6] (repositories)

A good deal is said in other chapters about structural, security and environmental aspects of the storage areas. This section addresses some practicalities.

(a) Modern media

In some cases general-purpose repositories (ill-advisedly) still make no separate provision for the storage of what BS 5454 terms 'modern media' (photographic, audio-visual and computer-readable documents), but instead leave them to take their chance in the general storage environment. More commonly, efforts are now widely being made to provide cooler, drier environments in accordance with national standards, either in separate rooms or in refrigerated units within another room. But quite a proportion of general repositories still report difficulties, for example in sufficiently reducing the relative humidity in a cool room, and in almost every case such rooms have taken a great deal longer to acclimatise than the general purpose strongrooms. Some archive services, as an alternative, have standing arrangements to transfer audio-visual material to specialist regional film and sound archives, which on the whole have fared better in this respect.

Film Archives – In the first arrangement of its kind, Norfolk County Council has entered into partnership with the University of East Anglia to house the Norfolk Record Office and the East Anglian Film Archive side by side in the same building, with dedicated storage and

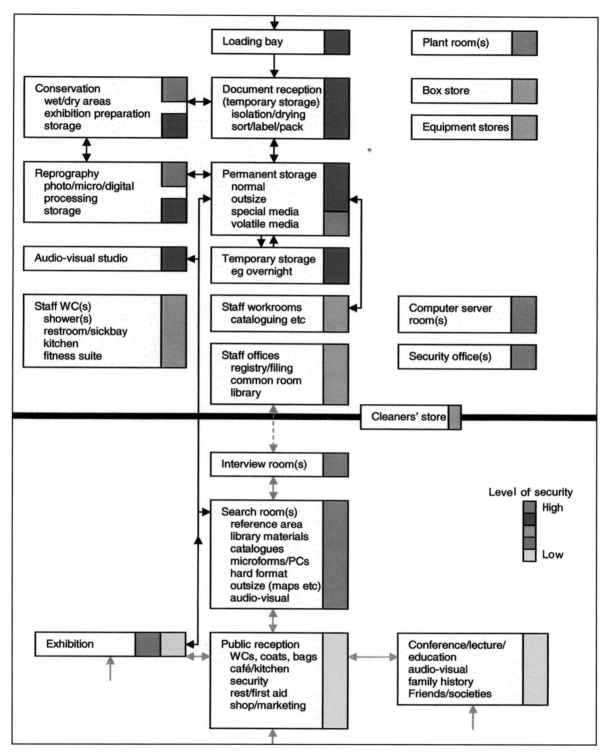

Fig 4 *Relationship of functions. Matching colours represent suggested comparable degrees of security. Black/ red arrows indicate flow of documents/public. Thick black line the limit of public access.*

public search facilities for each. Meanwhile the
Northern Region Film and TV Archive at the
University of Teesside, the North West Film
Archive at Manchester Metropolitan University,
and the Yorkshire Film Archive at the College
of York St John (see case study: Film Archives)
have each built new, state-of-the-art storage
facilities in this period. The National Screen
and Sound Archive of Wales has new premises
within the National Library.

Acclimatisation – For study, whether by staff
or public, archives move between two or more
different environments: respectively those in
the storage areas, in transit, and in the place of
consultation. In order to minimise any stress
on the materials, it is beneficial if they can be
allowed to adjust to their new environments
gradually, for example by passing through
acclimatisation rooms.

This is particularly critical in the case of any
photographic or film materials that have been
stored, as recommended, at cold temperatures,
where a sudden change might result in
condensation forming on the surface of the
carrying medium, or in mechanical damage if
they have lost some of their plasticity in cold
storage. At the English Heritage National
Monuments Record repository, all materials
in transit from the cold storage to the reading
rooms (and back) pass through special
acclimatisation chambers where, for a long
period overnight, the temperature and relative
humidity are changed very slowly to match
those on the other side. Other film archives
tend to have a number of separately climatised
rooms, each adjusted to the needs of specific
materials, and it is sometimes possible to move
material in transit gradually from the coolest
to the warmest space (and back). Only a few
general purpose record repositories make
separate provision for acclimatisation, although
in a few cases there are intermediate control
rooms between the storage and the reading
rooms where acclimatisation can to some
extent take place.

Regularly used paper and parchment
documents rarely get this treatment, largely
on the practical grounds that readers expect
a prompt service and in a busy repository
there is neither space nor time to add another
stage to the production process. This may not
strictly be in the best interests of the archives,
but it is inevitable in the real world. BS 5454

*Acclimatisation chambers, National Monuments
Record*

therefore suggests that the storage temperature
for these materials be kept at the upper end
of the recommended range (ie between 16
and 19°C), which is as near as possible to the
reading room environment. Infrequently used
materials can be stored at lower temperatures
but should then preferably be acclimatised
before consultation.

Faraday cage – Among the new buildings
considered, the National Library of Wales is
the only one to have lined one of its storage
units with copper foil, as a Faraday Cage to
protect magnetic media from being wiped
clean.[7]

(b) Large documents

Large documents including maps and plans
are sometimes also stored in separate rooms. It

Faraday cage, National Library of Wales

may be an advantage to have these as near to the search room (or lift) as possible, in order to reduce logistical difficulties in transporting them.

(c) Safe room(s)

Some repositories (eg the British Library and University College London) set aside a room with a greater degree of security for the storage of more valuable or confidential items.

(d) Volatile records

Cellulose nitrate film can ignite spontaneously. It is best not to house it in a general purpose archive repository at all, but to make special off-site arrangements. The Norfolk Record Office/East Anglia Film Archive has a small detached store for this purpose. English Heritage's National Monuments Record repository has a series of small vaults within the main building, but separated structurally from the main stores.

(e) Temporary storage

It is useful to designate specific secure space adjacent to the search room for holding documents on call until they are required. With appropriate environmental controls this may also assist them to acclimatise between the differing environments of the strongroom and the search room.

(f) Wooden racking

Opinion is divided on the merits of wooden racking. The basic requirement of BS 5454 (s.9.1.2) is that the material should be 'durable and non-combustible'. It used to be thought quite straightforward that metal was always preferable, and wood to be avoided because it was flammable and might give out acids which would harm the archival materials or react with metals such as lead in papal bulls or window lights and metallic silver in photographs. On the other hand wood of a suitable quality and thickness and appropriately treated is both sturdy and durable. If treated with flame-retardant, it will tend in the event of fire to smoulder for a considerable time before igniting. It can also be sealed (though not with an inflammable oil) to prevent acids leaching out, and that risk may be further lessened by storing the archives in acid-free boxes. In the previous volume a case was reported of a library which had a mixture of wooden and metal racking and was unfortunate enough to suffer a fire. The metal racking buckled in the heat and collapsed, whilst the wooden racking although charred remained intact. Many archive buildings do in fact rely on wooden or wood-product shelving. The only safe advice is to review the choice in the light of the overall strategy on fire and environmental control.

(g) Mobile racking[8]

Where floor-loadings permit, and funds run to it, most new repositories employ mobile racking for preference in order to maximise the use of storage space. This needs to be planned from the start, to take account of the floor-loading capacity of the structure. The size and shape of the storage area is best discussed in detail with shelving manufacturers, who will advise on the most cost-effective use of the space but may need reminding of the specific requirements of BS 5454 about racking, including the need to allow appropriate space for air circulation and for cleaning and maintenance. Mobile racking, although considerably more expensive than static shelving, can achieve significant savings in the use of space.

The 2000 edition of BS 5454 (unlike the preceding editions) avoided any particular

recommendation on shelving height, whilst
drawing attention to health and safety of staff
(s.9.2.3), an issue which has now been taken
further in the Work at Height Regulations
2005.[9] With suitable precautions in this
regard, several repositories including London
Metropolitan Archives, the Guardian/Observer
and Surrey have opted for very high racking
(from 3.5 m to as high as 4.9 m). In those
fortunate cases where there is no shortage of
space for lateral expansion, and/or where space
is not particularly expensive, this may not be
an issue, at least for the time being.

In a few cases, such as Glasgow University,
mobile racking has been installed on a special
bed that can be marginally adjusted to
compensate for any deflection. The Borthwick
Institute for Archives is pioneering the use of
electronic mobile racking.

Problems reported include:

- (in one instance) racking rolling of
  its own accord, corrected only at
  considerable expense by fitting motors to
  the units

- racking installed over a floor that was still
  drying out and having to be removed and
  re-fitted to correct warping in the floor

- water from a leak in the air-conditioning
  system collecting under a suspended floor
  carrying mobile racking, which had to be
  decanted and re-fitted

- inaccurate measurement of the shelving
  height or width, with the result that fewer
  archives than expected fitted into the
  available space

(h) Space for plant
Above the racking, whether static or mobile,
sufficient space must be allowed to facilitate
ventilation and/or allow for the installation
of any necessary trunking and services for
air handling and fire suppression. Calculating
the space required, and the knock-on effects
on shelving capacity, has sometimes proved
difficult.

Problems reported include:

- inaccurate measurement of the clearance
  between racking on the one hand and
  light fittings, air handling plant etc on the
  other

- inaccurate calculation of the quantity of
  air handling services, so that extra ducts
  had to be installed which look unsightly
  and take up a large amount of space.

(i) Emergency communications
All storage areas, especially those in which
people might be working alone, should
be provided with telephones for use in an
emergency. Another problem, specific to a
windowless strongroom, is total darkness in
the event of a power failure. To overcome
this, emergency lighting should be provided,
including as necessary rechargeable torches. In
some cases a luminous strip has been attached
to the end of each system of racking, or in a
line on the floor, to mark the way to the exit.

Staff room(s) for production and delivery of documents

Larger repositories will normally require a
room or rooms adjacent to the storage area(s)
to accommodate the staff who control the
production and delivery of documents.

Conservation workshop

The United Kingdom's archive repositories
are justifiably renowned for their conservation
services, and are the envy of many in the
museum and library world who have no in-
house facilities. Many conservators have now
designed their own workshops.

The most important considerations for a
conservation workshop are that it should,
be safe, comfortable to work in, conforming
with the Control of Substances Hazardous
to Health regulations, and ergonomically
efficient so that work moves smoothly from
one piece of equipment to the next in logical
sequence. Orientation is also important: in
the UK north-facing rooms will offer an even
light quality and preclude direct exposure to
sunlight. Presses and other heavy equipment
require substantial floor-loadings. The
checklist of essential services includes plenty
of power points; sink(s) and running water
with associated drainage services all preferably
sited on outside walls and fitted with external
overflows to prevent any mishap in the
workshop; and a safe system for the extraction
of fumes.

Ample storage space is required for
materials, and lockable storage for chemicals.

Generous space is desirable not only for the work-benches but for circulation around them, to cater for the full complement of staff and equipment projected over the lifetime of the building, but also to allow for the preparation and assembly of exhibitions, the repair of unusually large documents, and space for training demonstrations.

Several model layouts have been published,[10] and a number of permutations are possible. But success depends in part on the size, shape and orientation of the premises. Among the issues to be addressed are the separation of wet from dry processes, either in distinct rooms, or by flood sills as at the Borthwick Institute; and the extent to which the conservation workshop should be isolated from or integrated with, other functions. At Berkshire, for example, in order to integrate this function as closely as possible with the other offices there is no door separating the workshop from the adjacent open-plan office. Devon's occupancy of a very large warehouse enabled it to provide an enviably spacious conservation workshop. At the other end of the scale, in a confined space at Girton College Cambridge, three small rooms, one behind the other, have been provided to separate the different conservation processes.

Problems reported include:

- insufficient wall space for storage, wall-boards etc in rooms with too many windows

- wrong orientation, resulting in too much light at certain times of day.

Reprographics, digitisation etc[11]

The extent to which reprography is undertaken in-house varies considerably from repository to repository. Some contract out the reprographics service entirely. Facilities to be considered for any check-list include **camera room**(s), **dark room**(s), where a water supply will be required, **microfilm room**(s), **digitisation room**(s), **work and rest space** for the staff, and sufficient **storage** space for chemicals and materials.

Perhaps the greatest challenge in this period has been the steady growth of digitisation and in some places a commensurate (even total) reduction in photography. Rooms have had to be adapted, and additional space found, to meet this new demand.

Other storage and service space

Further storage space, in separate rooms or cupboards, is needed for boxes and packing materials, stationery stores, and cleaning materials respectively. This, unfortunately, is another amenity commonly sacrificed when budgets run thin.

Computer/server rooms

In a few instances, rooms have been specially designed to house the central computer, servers and related equipment. Where these are provided attention need to be paid to ventilation and temperature control.

Offices for professional and ancillary staff

Staff offices are the regular working environment and should take into account the individual's need for designated territory, the right balance between isolation when required (for example for interviews and confidential discussions) and awareness of the surrounding environment both inside and outside the building. In the latter respect a view from the windows may help. An adequate flow of fresh air should be ensured, and openable windows are an asset in this regard unless the building is located next to a source of external noise such as a busy street. Staff offices should not double as the staff tea-room.

Managers generally require their own reasonably sound-proof rooms, not a shared room or part of an open-plan office. Such rooms may need to be large enough for small meetings. At less senior levels, sharing of offices among staff remains common and in some cases is preferred. In larger offices separate space may need to be allocated for secretarial and administrative support staff and filing.

Problems reported include:

- lack of a room for confidential staff interviews

- the staff offices and tea room all in one, with continual distraction

- offices too small to take all the staff and volunteers on the complement, especially where additional people have been taken on on short-term contracts for specific projects.

Staff library

Larger repositories with considerable holdings of reference books for staff use, as in the national repositories or those housing another organisation such as a record society, family history society or the Victoria County History, have sometimes designated special rooms as libraries.

Other staff facilities

Other amenities may be needed, such as staff **showers** for use after work on dirty documents, and **first aid/rest rooms** equipped at the minimum with a bed and a wash basin, and located as near as possible to a WC. A few large repositories including TNA have recreational facilities including a small **gym**. Many more have a **staff tea room** and/or **kitchen** where staff and volunteers not on duty can take meal breaks. In all but the smallest repositories, the staff are normally provided with **WC and washroom** facilities separate from those used by the public. Where, exceptionally, these have to be located in common parts of a shared building, they can be kept private by means of a combination lock.

Plant

As hinted above, plant rooms need to be isolated from other functions to protect against fire and flood. It is preferable to locate plant not below, beside or above the storage areas, but separated from them, either in a detached building (as at Norfolk), or separated at least by a corridor and vented through an outside wall. But in practice this is often impossible on space or cost grounds. Some smaller repositories have air handling plant attached to outside walls (as at Tameside) or in inspection bays just inside the outer walls (Girton College Cambridge, and Hertfordshire). A common solution is to place at least some of the plant on the roof (as at Oxfordshire) or inside a separate top floor of the building, in effect inside the roof space (as at Berkshire, Devon and London Metropolitan Archives). Where this is done, it is normal to fit both fire- and water-detectors and alarms (since these areas may be left unattended for long periods), and there should be appropriate structural

precautions such as fire walls and tanking to prevent trouble spreading to any other part of the building in the event of a malfunction. Where water tanks and boilers have to be sited adjacent to, and on a level with, the storage areas, additional precautions will be necessary, including perhaps the installation of flood sills or drains next to the strongroom doors. Plant rooms should be fully secured at all times against unauthorised entry, and as access to plant rooms may be required outside normal office hours, it is preferable that they be accessible separately from the outside of the building rather than from the inside via other functions. It should also be remembered that parts of the equipment will wear out and have to be replaced from time to time, and this should be borne in mind when siting the plant room. Regular maintenance of plant is essential, to ensure its efficient operation and the elimination of risks from the contamination of the air by harmful organisms.

Several repositories have heating provided from a detached boiler unit. Within the repository, heating and water and electrical services including computer cabling might be carried in the wall space to minimise risks to the records. Wherever possible, in order to conserve energy, plant supplying hot water should be located close to the relevant service points. Individual water heaters might be considered as an alternative in washrooms and kitchens.

In converted buildings inherited services require special vigilance.

In some cases it can be necessary to install dedicated electricity sub-stations to serve the repository and guarantee a steady power supply.

Problems reported include:

- steam escaping from a boiler room located immediately next to the storage and with a connecting door, and filling the (fortunately then empty) store with steam and condensation;

- plant room squeezed into too small a space with the result that it is not easily accessed for maintenance;

- plant room on a roof, making the replacement of heavy parts problematic.

PUBLIC AREAS

Ideally, users of the archive service should be consulted at the planning stage about the kind of services they require, even if space or financial constraints in practice limit what can be achieved.

Reception

In the best modern designs the public enter the building through a unique and well-signed entrance. Many of the buildings featured in this book have a staffed **reception area** where readers sign in, apply for admission tickets if necessary, and ask preliminary questions. It is normal to include, off or adjacent to this area, the public **WCs** and **cloakrooms** or **lockers** for coats and bags, and any **common-room** or sitting-out area for the public. For many readers, research time is hard-earned and their breaks need to be as short as possible, so it is now established good practice for archive buildings to include a **refreshment area** where readers may either buy food and drink or eat their own food, make cups of tea or coffee or at the minimum buy drinks from a vending machine in order to avoid having to leave the building to find these services.

Among other services associated with the reception area, space is sometimes provided, as at Oxfordshire, for the display and **sale of publications,** or for a more general **information** and **sales-point.**

Problems reported include:

- in a small office, the labour-intensive nature of having a separate reception point

- isolation of staff working alone in the reception area.

Access for disabled people

Facilities for disabled people, both in the approach to the building, at the door and within the reception area, have widely been improved in line with the Disability Discrimination Act 1995. Detailed and specific guidance has been issued for libraries in this period, which applies with equal force to archives.[12] It affects the planning of doors, steps/ramps, lifts and WCs, the height of tables and chairs, colour contrasts in décor and on computer screens, and many other features. (All this applies to the other public areas of the building also.) In converted buildings access for the disabled is not always so easy to achieve, and this needs careful thought when considering building options.

Problems reported include:

- staff desks too high for disabled people to see over (eg on a daïs)

- door handles/door openings, even on a disabled lift, wrongly sited for wheelchair users.

Exhibition area[13]

Exhibitions are always popular with visitors and attract a wider public than just the regular readers. Increasingly the practice is to site an exhibition area in or near reception in order to make it as accessible as possible to the general public without increasing disturbance elsewhere in the building. BS 5454 deals with exhibitions in some detail (s.13). It emphasises that wherever original records as distinct from reproductions are displayed, security, environmental and lighting controls should match those in the permanent storage areas. The area may require special security alarms and adequate means of invigilation, perhaps with the use of CCTV if the area is not permanently staffed, ultra-violet screens and/or blinds for the windows (if any), unimpeded wall space and room for free-standing screens or display cases.

Spacious new exhibition areas have been provided, in the national sector by the British Library, TNA and the National Library of Wales, in university repositories including those at London Metropolitan University's Women's Library, Nottingham, Southampton and York, and in a number of local repository archives, where the most striking example is that at Norfolk, where visitors walk through a long exhibition gallery on the way to the reading rooms. Business and specialist repositories sometimes also have exhibition areas. At the Guardian/Observer Newsroom a remarkable degree of adaptability has been provided, with suspended screens that stow away when not required. At St George's Chapel, Windsor, a useful new exhibition space was included in the conversion.

Problems reported include:

- fixed cases positioned on the floor, reducing flexibility for successive exhibitions

- wall materials such as brick that cannot be penetrated for hanging

- noise from hard or polished floors and walls

- display cases angled in such a way or at such a height that the contents cannot be seen from a wheelchair.

Search room[14]

see also Ch.5 Security

For most visitors this room is the main port of call. Improved standards of decor, lighting, furniture and carpeting, are everywhere contributing to a more comfortable working environment. Decorations and furnishings in light tones, not so strikingly bright as to be a distraction,[15] but not gloomy either, provide a calm and pleasant setting. Carpets, curtains and noise-absorbing ceiling materials also help to minimise disturbance. Lighting needs to be so appointed as to reduce glare while providing adequate ambient light for reading. Where computers are likely to be used for research, requisitioning, or access to on-line data, adequate provision needs to be made not only for the cabling and power supplies (also increasingly wireless-enabled facilities), but also for the space occupied by the equipment.

Academic researchers in particular like the search room to be quiet,[16] and need plenty of space. Family historians on the other hand often have a less silent, more gregarious approach, and some effort is often made to cater for these divergent needs.

Some, like Denbighshire, the National Library of Wales and Surrey, dedicate a separate reference room to the consultation of online and/or hard copy catalogues, indexes and other finding aids as well as personal enquiries about the records, in order to concentrate this potentially noisy activity in one place, at one stage removed from the search room. Sometimes, as at Leeds University and Essex what is in effect a single room has been divided by one or more glazed partitions to separate these and other functions. Smaller record offices may have no need for this degree of segregation, but it is gaining favour, sometimes with a common staff service point straddling the frontier to enable a degree of service and invigilation on both sides. Reference areas, as well as the search room, may require some invigilation since

finding aids, and particularly printed reference works, both of which may be irreplaceable, are prone to wander or be removed without authority. Where local studies libraries are an integral part of the service, magnetic or radio-frequency book alarm systems have sometimes been installed at the exit.

Depending on the scale of the operation, the nature of the holdings, and again on local practice, distinct areas if not distinct rooms can be provided for the respective consultation of **microfilm**, traditional media (records on paper and parchment), and **out-size documents** especially **maps**. This however can present staffing, managerial and logistical problems, with readers perhaps coming and going across each other's paths and requiring assistance and/or invigilation in several separate areas simultaneously. Microfilm and digitised holdings are growing fairly generally, and this shift in the pattern of use needs to be taken into account when apportioning space.

Problems reported include

- tables and chairs for public use being of a fixed height which does not suit everyone, especially when it comes to the consultation of microforms and online material

- supply of end-of-range furniture which cannot be replaced like for like

- lighting permanently too dim or too bright.

Where audio-visual records are held, appropriate **listening/viewing facilities** should also be provided, as at Norfolk, although in practice this has not always been done. Similarly where readers are permitted to use computers or tape-recorders special provision should be made, including the necessary cabling and sound-proof cubicles if required.

An interview room is occasionally provided, in which readers on their first visit or with particularly detailed research problems may meet a member of the professional staff. Cubicles whose walls do not extend to the full ceiling height (above any suspended ceiling) are not likely to be effectively soundproof.

Public meeting rooms

Policies and programmes for outreach and public relations vary considerably from one authority to another. Pressure is mounting, especially owing to the growing educational demand for access to original sources for study, for **seminar, lecture** and/or **classroom** facilities. Access to any such rooms (and perhaps to any self-service family history rooms as at the Borthwick Institute) should be either from the main reception area or by means of a separate outer door so that the room(s) can be used outside normal opening hours without giving admittance to the archive repository. A self-contained unit for these public functions, with its own access and WCs, is clearly the best solution. If it is intended to produce original documents in the meeting rooms, for example for teaching purposes, it will be helpful to locate them as near as possible to the strongroom area, or to have a small strongroom adjacent, to house documents securely on a temporary basis.

Raked lecture theatres with modern sound and projection equipment have been provided in a number of repositories including Essex, the Guardian/Observer and the National Library of Wales, and large meeting rooms with level floors in many others including Norfolk and York University's Borthwick Institute. In the latter approach, it is an advantage to have movable and preferably stackable furniture to allow the rooms to be used flexibly.

Meeting rooms intended for multiple purposes can also usefully incorporate stacking space for chairs and tables, and lockable storage space for audio-visual and other equipment. Where such outreach is intended, it may be advantageous to provide a separate, sound-proofed and suitably equipped **education room**, with appropriate ancillary space for **storage** of materials and equipment, and if applicable the accommodation of the **education officer**.

Cleaners' store

The regular cleaners will, at the minimum, need storage space, and depending on the duration of their work possibly also an office or sitting area.

Expansion space

Not included on the flow diagram, but very definitely to be taken into account when planning, is the question of expansion space for the future, for all functions and services where an increased demand for space is to be expected.

Appendix to Chapter 2[17]
Headings towards a brief for an archive building
Overall considerations

The current state of play including:

- agreements and understandings already reached, budget commitments
- reasons why the new building is needed
- budgetary, timing and other constraints
- possible alternative strategies.

The records held/to be held:

- their nature
- their use (by whom, for what purposes).

Standards:

Compliance with:

- BS 5454 and other relevant British Standards for specific media.
- TNA's Standard for record repositories and Framework of Standards.

In particular:

- the priority to be given to the secure custody of the records
- their protection against fire and flood, damp and heat, atmospheric and environmental pollution, dust, insects and vermin, unauthorised access and all other hazards
- stability of the internal environment within approved ranges.

Strategies and policy directives

The authority's commitment to, or the building's need to comply with, other national, regional or local policy directives, on matters such as:

- environmental issues including regeneration, transport
- energy consumption
- value for money, including Whole Life Costing (ease of maintenance, management, communication)
- access for disabled people
- health and safety.

The broad groups of functions to be housed in the building, and the desirability of separating archive storage from other functions.

The main considerations affecting choice of site, structure and materials.

Overall ambience, style and impact on the community.

Any specific problems of the existing service which it is hoped will be overcome in the new building.

Overall statistics of present and projected use, such as:

- quantity of records held now/rate of accrual in recent years
- number of records produced for inspection in a given time span (eg a year)
- number of public visits eg per day, per week, and their typical duration; recent overall trends; maximum to be provided for
- number of staff employed/to be employed
- need for car parking space, and impact of road access on local traffic
- expected duration of occupancy of new building/provision for expansion
- total floor space required (broken down by function below).

Any predictable changes in the nature or media of holdings or pattern of their accrual or use during the lifespan of the building.

Individual functions and their relationship

For each function identified in the checklist:
Space required[18]
    area/volume, special dimensional requirements, headroom, storage space expansion space
Nature of the activities:
    Special statutory or other requirements eg Health & Safety
Structural requirements:
    floor-loading; orientation; provision/absence of windows compartmentation
General ambience:
    colour scheme; comfort; noise levels/acoustics.
Security, flood and fire precautions, pest control
Environmental controls:
    temperature relative humidity ventilation air quality, filtration lighting
Communications:
    links to other functions
    telecommunications
    computer
Services:
    power supply; number and location of points; isolation water supply; location of services and drainage; sanitation; location and route of services
Furniture, equipment and machinery.

Chapter 3

THE SITE

(BS 5454:2000 s.4)

BS 5454:2000 offers guidance on the factors to be considered when selecting a site for an archive building. It is rare to find a site that is ideal in every respect. In practice some limitations and compromises usually have to be accepted, but this should be done in an informed way, after careful evaluation of any specific hazards associated with the site, and not simply in haste by a commissioning authority that has at best a vague notion of the purposes of an archive building or the needs of its users.

Why need so much care be taken over the choice of site? Apart from convenience for public access, factors such as the shape, geology, topography, ecology and environmental context of the site will determine the kind of building that can be constructed there and the materials to be used. And that in turn will make a critical contribution to the well-being of the archives to be housed there.

Fig.5 summarises the main hazards associated with the site.[1]

In order to isolate the building from all hazards in adjacent properties and give good all round access to the exterior for maintenance and for the emergency services, a detached and self-contained property is to be preferred. This should be taken into account when selecting a site. The land itself should not be contaminated. It must be capable of bearing the building and its contents without

Risk	Possible counter-indicators (new and converted buildings)
Restricted site	Building joined on to adjacent property Building shared with other occupants Insufficient space for expansion Difficult access for emergency services Difficult access for incoming documents
Subsidence	Adverse report by structural engineer Settlement cracks in existing building on site
Structural damage/ heavy maintenance	Site exposed to strong wind, strong sun, sea air Age of building Method of construction
Fire and explosion	Adjacent woodland, airport, military site, industrial premises, flammable stores including fuel tanks Appreciable distance from fire brigade
Flood and damp	Waterside site, low-lying ground, ground sloping steeply towards or beside site Necessity to use basement for storage
Dust and atmospheric pollution	Site adjacent to or down-wind of industrial processes, derelict or demolition sites, busy main roads, railway lines
Noise	Aircraft, road and rail traffic, industrial processes
Vandalism and crime	Isolated or partially concealed site Area known to be prone to vandalism or crime Adjacent waste land as source of projectiles Appreciable distance from police station or security centre No perimeter fence: exposure to damage or ram-raiding

Fig. 5 *Summary of risks associated with the site*

subsidence. The surrounding land and adjacent properties should present no obvious risk of fire or explosion, flood or damp, excessive dust or atmospheric pollution or, where magnetic media are to be stored, electro-magnetic interference. The site should not be in an area notorious for vandalism or crime. Proximity to the fire and police services could be an advantage, but ought not to be relied upon, since recent experience has shown that the number and location of these stations can be changed at short notice.

If a site raises important concerns under any of these headings, the first reaction need not always be to reject it out of hand. Instead, a cool-headed risk assessment should be carried out. How likely is it that the risk would materialise? How serious would the consequences be? Could the risk be eliminated, contained, or managed to the point that it became acceptable? Hazards are of course associated with every aspect of an archive building and its maintenance as well as merely with the site, so BS 5454:2000 pays particular attention to Risk Management. Unfortunately, some custodians and governing authorities may still be unaware of the risks they run or the need to manage them. Many – perhaps most – repositories are however managing and living with risks every day, as a number of the examples below will show.

- Some serious hazards such as earthquakes are fortunately uncommon in the United Kingdom, but not entirely unknown: the British Geological Survey's database was checked before The National Archives chose to deposit records in Deepstore's commercial storage in a Cheshire salt mine.

- The likelihood of an airliner crashing on a particular building is of course very small, and archive buildings cannot realistically be constructed to withstand such a catastrophe. But the likelihood is clearly increased if the site is directly under a flight path to an airport. In such cases, not just the relatively insignificant risk of a crash, but concomitant hazards such as noise and air pollution or parts falling off an aircraft, need to be considered. Rightly or wrongly, these hazards are being lived with daily, for example in TNA, the National Archives of Scotland (Thomas

Thomson House) and Devon Record Office.

- For many other site-associated hazards the history of the site and of previous use of the land could be instructive. Records might show, for example, any known incidence of flooding in the past century or more. But given the increasingly severe storms and flooding experienced locally throughout the United Kingdom in recent years, and the forecasts of worse to come through climate change, a significant safety margin over and above the highest recorded flood level to date should be factored in. Essex, Denbighshire and Shropshire Record Offices have all been on the edge of local floods since they were built. In Essex's case the advice of the National Rivers Authority had been taken on the 100-year flood level of the river, but this was inadequate when local drainage and flood control systems failed in an unfortunate, and one has to hope unrepeatable, incident.

- Orkney Library and Archives is another interesting case. As the land on which it is built was low-lying near the sea, and flooding of the site can by no means be ruled out, the archive services were as a precaution placed on the first floor. There were other complications too. The building was designed on paper to be oriented to give best protection against sun and wind and to maximise the potential for natural ventilation. At a late stage of the planning it was learnt that part of the anticipated site could not be acquired for development. To save major delay and expense in redesigning the whole building, it was decided to use the existing design but swing the building round by 90 degrees to fit the new site. This disturbed many of the assumptions about exposure to sun and wind and required a different approach to acclimatisation.

- In Carmarthenshire's case, a flash flood running downhill on the site conspired with blocked local drains to flood the building during conversion.

- A detailed risk assessment of the site for the Essex Record Office, before it was built on the site of a former gasworks, concluded that any contamination in the land was sufficiently contained.

- In historic towns and cities, and on other sites of likely archaeological significance, a preliminary site survey and possibly a dig might be necessary. The extension to York Minster Library, on a sensitive site within the city's Roman forum, had to be preceded by an archaeological investigation which affected the timing of the building project and then the nature of the building's foundations. A similar investigation at Hereford cathedral preceded the building of the new Library extension, when over 1,100 articulated human skeletons were unearthed.[2] The North West Film Archive found under its yard a cobbled quayside from the original canalside site on which its warehouse building stands. Building work on the East Riding's new Treasure House (still in progress at the time of this study) was held up for 4 months pending archaeological investigations.

- Underground streams have been found in a number of cases when preparing the foundations for archive buildings.

- Not only archaeological remains may lie beneath the surface. A high voltage power cable found during excavation for the foundations of the new building at the John Rylands University Library of Manchester had to be moved, resulting in a 4-month delay to the project.[3]

- Potentially dangerous neighbours to some of the new buildings visited include petrol stations and the chemistry department of a university.

At the most basic level the choice of a site, and the way it can be developed, might well be constrained even by the availability and cost of land for development, by national and local planning policies or strategies, and/or by building and environmental regulations. This will have knock-on consequences such as whether the building can be in a town centre and/or conveniently placed in relation to public transport and amenities such as shops and restaurants, or to related offices of the parent authority.

- Shropshire Records and Research Centre is built on a convenient town-centre site, connected to the adjacent library and just across the road from Shrewsbury railway station. However, the position, on a hillside, constrained the size and shape of the building and adversely affected the inter-relationship of some functions such as document reception and conservation.

- Essex Record Office and Greenwich Heritage Centre are among those whose location was influenced at least in part by a wider scheme to regenerate the area in question. In Essex's case, the wider regeneration scheme did not materialize and the record office is as a result relatively isolated.

- Worcestershire chose to develop a former department store in the heart of Worcester city centre for its new Family History Centre, mainly for ease of public access.

- Conversely, several major repositories have found rural or suburban, and not always readily accessible, sites to be the only available or the only affordable option (eg Diageo plc, National Archives of Scotland, Thomas Thomson House).

- The English Heritage National Monuments Record repository at Swindon is in a conservation area and had to be designed in such a way that important views of the adjacent listed buildings were not impeded. A glass link between the old and new buildings gives an impression of detachment, and the angled and curved design serves to reduce the visual impact of the building's mass.[4]

The relationship with the surrounding environment is a two-way concern: not only the effect that the surroundings will have on the archives, but also the effect that the archive building, when it goes up, will have on the environment. There is no reason why, with a careful choice of site, an archive building should not enhance rather than detract from its surroundings, and even serve a strategic purpose such as regeneration. So an **environmental impact assessment** is highly desirable before proceeding with a new building

Low level landscaping

on a given site. A repository with substantial storage capacity can bulk rather large in the landscape. If on top of that its predominant characteristic is unalleviated, featureless walls that make it look like an industrial warehouse, it may be an unwelcome newcomer in, for example, an otherwise residential neighbourhood. The aesthetic impact of archival buildings is a matter for consideration at the planning stage (*see the next chapter*), but the options will in part be determined by the context of the site.

Almost irrespective of location, **landscaping** (where practicable) with lawns, trees and shrubs has become increasingly popular as a means of improving the appearance of a site and softening the impact of an otherwise austere building upon the local environment. Small gardens in internal courtyards, tree-lined patios, or just potted shrubs and flowers, have all found their place, and have cheered up the working environment for all

concerned. The cost of gardening and other subsequent maintenance has, of course, to be taken into account. The provision of attractive surroundings for the building through landscaping has been a particular feature in many places. Among many good examples might be cited The National Archives, the British Library, the National Monuments Record and Shropshire Record Office. Any landscaping must, however, be undertaken with one eye on risk management: trees and shrubs should not be planted in such a way as to provide a hiding place for an intruder or facilitate access to windows, and it should also be borne in mind that they might encourage insect or bird life, and therefore should not be sited near vents and openings. Another potential hazard is fire from tinder-dry plants.

Will the comings and goings of public and staff have an impact on the local community and its infrastructural needs (transport, traffic management, car parking, shops, etc)? At the planning stage it is important to inform and consult the local communities fully and to address any concerns. Will the same comings and goings, or anything else about the building, such as the operation of machinery (extractor fans, air-conditioning equipment), increase the noise and inconvenience to the neighbours, and how can this be minimised?

In short, for a variety of reasons the choice of site really does matter, and deserves careful thought. It has implications for much of the overall strategy on such matters as security, fire prevention and environmental control which are separately treated below, and it is one of the determinants of the kind of building that can or should emerge from the planning process.

Chapter 4

STRUCTURE AND MATERIALS

1. GENERAL CONSIDERATIONS[1]

Provided that everything about the building promotes their well-being, archives will outlive their present owners, custodians and readers, and with any luck their present accommodation as well. The aim is nothing less.

With that in mind, what sort of attributes or qualities do we expect of the structure of an archive building today, and what implications do these have for the choice of materials for its construction and fitting out?

Above all, the structure must be resistant to fire, and as secure as possible against unauthorised entry.

Beyond these two prime considerations we could do worse than adapt a set of attributes or 'conditions' which Bruce Allsopp suggested might reasonably be looked for by the occupier of *any* building: namely that it should be (a) structurally stable, (b) weatherproof and (c) a means of '[moderating] the climate for the comfort of people'; that it should achieve this

Stone: York Minster Library

(d) with low expenditure of energy, and (e) with economy in the use of scarce materials; and (f) should combine durability with low maintenance costs.[2] In the case of an archive building this vision must be interpreted as if the archives and not the people were the principal occupants.

It is worth looking at each of these general attributes in turn.

Fire resistance[3]
see also Chapter 6.

In new buildings, compliance with the general Building Regulations is of course the first necessary step in fire prevention, but this should be seen as a bare minimum standard: it is not in itself sufficient for archive storage, nor does such compliance convey immunity from risk, whether from fire and flood or on security grounds.[4]

In a repository which takes account of all BS 5454's other recommendations, the likelihood of a fire, even out of office hours, is extremely remote. Boxed and compactly stored paper does not readily ignite. On the other hand, once ablaze it may be lost irredeemably, so fire-proofing is still important in both new and converted buildings, and a high standard is now being consistently reached in the UK's archive buildings.

BS 5454:2000 reinstated the recommendation which had slipped out in 1989 that all materials used in walls, doors, floors and ceilings of an archive repository (ie the storage area) should offer four-hour fire resistance. This is double the 2-h resistance commonly encountered elsewhere in Europe,[5] and serves to underline the fact that in the case of archives we are dealing with irreplaceable material. Four-hour resistance is certainly achievable in new buildings – of course at a cost. In some converted buildings it is unattainable because of the nature of the given structure. Anything less than 4-h resistance should only be contemplated if the overall fire-protection strategy is sufficiently robust (for example if

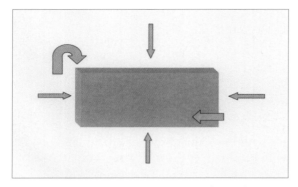

Fig. 6 *All-round protection against fire and water*

it combines incipient-fire detection and an automatic fire-suppression system),[6] and if the level of risk has been minimised in the light of a full risk assessment.

The importance of *all-round* protection against fire (Fig. 6) needs emphasising. Four-hour walls alone are not a panacea if, say, the archives are housed above other functions whose ceiling has a lower fire-rating and might be the first thing to collapse in the event of a fire, or if the doors are of a weak fire-rating or are not tight fitting.[7] Any identified weak spots should be reinforced. For example steel roller shutters might be added to existing strongroom doors. This has been done even in some new buildings, Essex and Surrey among others. However, there is little point in this if the walls themselves do not have a strong fire-rating. Or, to take another instance, a mineral fire retardant might, if so recommended by the fire service, be added to ceilings to improve their fire rating, as at Southampton University Library.

Roof lights, TNA

From the point of view of fire resistance, brick, stone and reinforced concrete are the materials of choice for the construction of archive buildings, especially for the outer shell of the building and the shell of the storage areas. Steel and other metals liable to conduct heat throughout the structure in the event of a serious fire (or even to buckle and collapse) of course have to be used, for example in the frame, but some caution is necessary.[8] In particular, metal uprights that support racking should not be integral to the structure of the building (as is sometimes the case in older library buildings like Manchester City Archives). In new buildings, timber and other combustible materials, including flammable finishes and fixtures, should be kept to a minimum in accordance with BS 5454. Vigilance on this last point is advisable when selecting a building for conversion.

In order to prevent the spread of both smoke and fire, new repositories with air-conditioning are mostly equipped with self-closing ducts, vents and fire doors (BS 5454 s.6.5). In this context, too, the siting and number of doors, windows, corridors, stairwells and lifts is important. Lift shafts are as good as chimneys for providing oxygen to sustain a fire. This, in addition to security, is a reason why lifts should not be so located as to open directly into storage areas. On the other hand, a sturdy lift is an asset not to be lightly spurned, and where no other solution is possible – in a converted warehouse, for example – it might be possible to encase the lift shaft within fire-resistant walls and equip it with special fire doors, as was noted at Bristol in the previous volume.

Fire and smoke are more likely to occur in parts of the building other than the repository, so careful attention needs to be paid to the overall fire-protection strategy for the building, and to the extraction of smoke which might penetrate into the repository even from a fire seated elsewhere. In the event of a fierce fire flammable gases can accumulate at the top of the affected space and result in the phenomenon known as 'flash-over' in which they ignite suddenly and intensify the conflagration, as was found in the Norwich fire of 1994.[9] The National Archives building at Kew has roof windows in the glazed atria of its staff and public areas which open automatically in the event of fire, both in order to prevent flash-over and to assist with smoke

Lakeland slate: Jerwood Centre

extraction. Smoke extract vents are a notable feature of the walls of Thomas Thomson House (National Archives of Scotland).

In determining the structural defences against fire it must also be remembered that in an emergency the brigade must have access.[10] The Norwich experience suggests that it is also important to allow ample, unobstructed space immediately inside doors, and generous main gangways to assist both entry and evacuation in an emergency.

Compartmentation?

BS 5454: 2000, whilst acknowledging (s.5.3.3) that compartments may be advantageous, makes no specific recommendation with regard to their size, whether for fire protection or other purposes.[11] This is to allow for differences between repositories in a number of variables, for example:

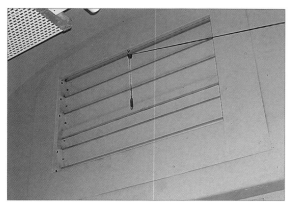

Smoke vents, NAS

- the scale of their operations and holdings;

- management and staff preferences for ease of access to, and freedom of circulation within, storage areas; and, most particularly

- the strategy chosen for fire protection/ suppression.

In a converted building the compartmentation may come as a given.

Whatever the size of compartments, they need to be of no lower fire rating than that of the main repository structure. Small compartments are easier to isolate in the event of fire, and have long been advocated for library stacks as well as for archives. Compartments can also help to limit a flood or infestation to one particular 'cell' without endangering holdings stored away from the source of the problem. They might also be required if a gas-based fire-suppression system is to be installed which requires a sealed space of limited volume to operate effectively: on this point the manufacturer's advice should be sought.

Compartments are much less necessary where a water-sprinkler system is installed whose heads can address a fire in a specific location. A multiplicity of very small storage areas, can be difficult to acclimatise evenly without replicating plant and equipment in many rooms. Walls will take up a lot of the available footprint so that the total space available might not be as generous as it appears on paper. Management and security can be more complex in a highly-compartmented repository (more doors to be checked for security, more to be opened and closed for the retrieval of documents, and so on). These issues have had to be grappled with in places such as the former gaol used by Denbighshire Record Office and the former university hall of residence used by the Museum of English Rural Life at Reading University (which has in excess of 30 store rooms).

Security

see also Chapter 5.

After fire-resistance, security looms especially large in any consideration of structure and materials. In both new and converted archive buildings attention must be paid to the dimensions and materials of all openings in the shell – doors, windows, vents, chimneys, inspection hatches, etc – and to external features such as window ledges, buttresses, drainpipes and fire-escape ladders, which might variously invite unauthorised entry, afford concealment or assist an intruder's climb to upper levels.

Among specific points worth emphasising from the experience of archive buildings:

- Drainpipes should be located beyond the reach of windows, or recessed within small buttresses to make them impossible to climb.

- Bars or grilles on windows should be incorporated into the masonry, preferably on the inside. One building in this period had external bars on its office windows prised apart by thieves using a hydraulic tool and intent on stealing computer equipment.

- Exposed windows should be of reinforced laminated glass and not louvred.

- External roller-shutters should be heavy-duty, not lightweight, nor should they be fitted in such a way that they can be hauled off their mountings.

Terrorist bomb or incendiary attacks which can pose a threat to public buildings have unfortunately continued to occur from time to time during this period. They have sometimes been taken into account in the structure, design and security of archive buildings. One repository which holds potentially sensitive archival material has had its strongroom walls specially reinforced against the possibilities of bomb blast or ram-raiding, which may be an issue especially in town centres.

Structural stability

It is self-evident that strong foundations are among the first requisites of any building, but this is not something that can be taken for granted. In converted buildings which have not already been used for heavy storage the nature of the foundations has to be tested. For new buildings the nature of the foundations required will depend mainly on the geology and/or the previous use of the site, and on whether static or mobile racking is proposed.

Archives are surprisingly heavy. Averages are not specially helpful because the materials are very variable in size and mass, but according to one calculation[12] the average weight of a metre-

run of documents is around 50 kg excluding the shelf, and for large volumes may reach 90 kg. Floor-loadings, at every level where archives are to be stored, and also in other rooms which are to house heavy equipment such as conservation presses, boilers or water tanks, have to take account of the stresses which will be exerted when the building is fully occupied.

BS 5454 (s 5.9) recommends, for evenly distributed loads of static racking, a floor-loading of at least 10-12 kiloNewtons per square metre. Mobile shelving uses storage space more efficiently than static, but thereby concentrates the load for a given floor area and requires greater floor-loading capacity. So the Standard recommends that manufacturers be consulted on likely loads before it is installed.

Weatherproofing/protection against water damage

The shell of an archive building must serve to buffer the contents against all external forces: lightning and tempest, of course, but also the regular forces of sun, rain and wind, heat and cold, and daily variations in relative humidity.

The overall exposure of the building should be taken into account when determining the site. Jersey Archive is unusually well protected, from strong winds in particular, by being located in the bed of a former stone quarry. Orkney Library and Archives on the other hand, at the other geographical extremity of this study, is in a relatively exposed situation at low level near the sea.

Exposure to the sun, bringing the risk of increased temperature in the repository owing to the transmission of heat through the roof and walls, can be mitigated by the choice of materials and degree of insulation, and by features such as roof overhangs to shade the upper walls. To shade the lower parts of the walls the judicious planting of shrubs or creepers has sometimes been the solution adopted, although short-term risks from this might include the inadvertent provision of a place for an intruder to lurk, and long-term risks possible damage to the fabric through the attachment of climbing plants. This is a separate issue from the more general (and desirable) landscaping referred to above, which is undertaken for aesthetic or ecological reasons.

When it comes to protection against water, as with fire, all-round protection (Fig 6) is vital, whether the hazard arises from the weather outside or from bursts, spillages and leakages inside. Once again, the basic structure can assist, and this may need to be taken even more seriously in future if we are to expect heavier rainfall and more powerful storms, as seems likely.[13] Other features such as tanking and water alarms are dealt with below, and some water hazards can be eliminated by the careful placing of functions requiring water, and by ensuring that no water pipes pass through the repository unless specifically needed. New buildings are sadly not immune from leaks. The completion and handover of a number of new repositories including Lancaster University's Ruskin Library, was among those held up pending remedial work.[14]

Drainage

Attention also needs to be paid to good drainage, both outside and inside the building. In many new buildings, among them Devon, Churchill Archive Centre Cambridge, Southampton University Library, Unilever, and the Borthwick Institute at York, special attention has been paid to internal drainage, to reduce the risk of flooding from any source. In Oxfordshire, glass tiles in the floor can be blown out if emergency drainage is required. Any drains inside the building should be fitted with one-way valves to allow flood water, or water released during fire-fighting, to escape but not to rise. A storage area which is itself well protected from water will be put at risk if water could accumulate undrained in the adjacent corridor.[15] It is surprising how

Drain outside strongroom, Devon

frequently the need for internal drains is still overlooked.

Flood water presents threats not only of damp but also of contamination by biological or chemical agents.[16] As already noted, serious external flooding has threatened a number of archive buildings in this period. Despite all precautions a number of more minor floods and leaks have also been reported throughout the country, even in new buildings, after occupancy but fortunately almost entirely in public rather than storage areas, arising from causes such as defective gutters and blocked drains (including at least two cases of birds' nests or dead birds being washed into unprotected gutters or drains and causing a blockage), or from internal mishaps such as leaking kitchen pipes, or overflowing dehumidifiers or WCs. Risk assessments have increasingly led to counter-measures such as the tanking of floors, and installation of flood-alarms.

The use of basement accommodation, especially in or near an area at risk of flooding, should only be contemplated after a thorough risk assessment and appropriate counter-measures which, in new buildings or substantial *in situ* rebuilds on site, might include tanking, the provision of adequate damp-proofing, and drains or pumps with which to evacuate water quickly in any emergency. Tate Britain, where archives are stored in a basement below the level of the Thames, has a steel flood barrier door.

Drying out

The use of wet processes in construction necessarily means that the building will take a considerable time to dry out, and it is particularly important in the case of the archive storage areas that this process should have been fully completed before any seal is applied to the floors or the archives are moved in. Calculating the period required is notoriously difficult, but in many cases the strategy has been to build the repository first and allow it to dry out while other parts of the building are constructed. In Jersey, for example, the repository was allowed to dry out for a whole summer before being sealed up.

Problems reported include:

- At the Borthwick Institute in York something like a year was allowed for the drying process. At the end of that

Wet concrete (Photo: Hertfordshire Record Office)

time the fabric was still found to be holding residual moisture so industrial dehumidifiers were brought in to complete the drying.

- The drying-out period for a deep concrete floor may be much longer than expected. In one repository a floor covering was laid too soon, while the concrete was still drying out, and as a result the covering soon warped and cracked. This could only be remedied at considerable expense and inconvenience, involving the removal of the racking and re-laying of the floor covering.

- Because of time constraints, another repository had to install its racking on a floor that was still wet after being exposed to the elements during building.

Environmental control

Air-conditioning, separately considered in chapter 7, can be a valuable asset. But other countries which experience greater extremes of heat and cold than the United Kingdom and yet lack the resources to consider air-conditioning have long known how to live comfortably without it, relying instead on buildings of substantial mass to buffer the internal against the external environment, and developing other design features such as overhanging roofs to shade and shelter the walls, with minimal fenestration in walls which directly face a hot sun.[17] Similar attributes in the thick, stone-built muniment rooms of earlier centuries, have assisted the survival of medieval documents, again without recourse to any high-tech solutions.

Natural climatisation and high thermal inertia[18]

As already noted in the Introduction, this period has seen a marked growth in scientific research, both in the UK and overseas, into building materials and techniques which seek to stabilise temperature and relative humidity in archive storage areas without recourse to air-conditioning, and indeed with the minimum amount of intervention of any kind. Computer modelling software has been developed to take account of a number of variables ranging from the thermal properties of the building materials to typical local outdoor climatic conditions when calculating the likely range of indoor temperature and relative humidity for a given building.

Lars Christoffersen studied in depth the regional archive of Schleswig-Holstein in Germany, a building with high-density insulated walls and roof which was designed to be naturally acclimatised. From this he developed a theoretical model for application to other passive-climate-controlled repositories. His published research[19] showed that, allowing for a very slow seasonal drift up and down (a concept which is taken up in chapter 7), temperature was contained, at least in Schleswig's case, within the overall range 14.5 to 20.5°C, and relative humidity within the range 56 to 62 per cent.

In such a building, a substantial air cavity is typically placed behind the outer layer of masonry. Vents or air bricks in the outer walls admit fresh air to the cavity, allowing it to rise through the full height of the building and to circulate throughout the roof space, before escaping through further vents at that level. This is primarily to provide cooling. It has nothing to do with the ventilation of the inside of the repository, where indeed air changes are generally kept to a minimum or where (as in Jersey's case) air is admitted through controllable vents only very infrequently, when outside conditions are favourable.[20] Within public and staff areas, on the other hand, natural ventilation is encouraged, air being admitted through vents set low in the external walls, using pressure and heat differentials between one side of the building and the other to encourage its circulation and eventual extraction through vents set higher in the walls on the other side.

Whilst it is very much to be hoped that archive buildings in the UK can in future use natural climatisation processes to a greater degree, and thereby consume less energy, there are a number of difficulties with Christoffersen's model:

- Since chemical reactions accelerate in proportion to increases in temperature,[21] in the case of archives a cool storage temperature should ideally be maintained throughout the year. BS 5454 already makes some compromises with that ideal, allowing for some drift (*see chapter 7 below*), but it sets the recommended upper level for temperature at 19°C, which is significantly below that attainable in the model.

- If − and it is an 'if' − hotter summers are to be expected as a result of changing climatic patterns and global warming, temperatures in this kind of repository seem certain to peak in summer at an even higher level, from which (because of the building's very design) they will descend only slowly.

- Since building materials have different thermal coefficients, and every site its own specific exposure to wind and sun, separate calculations need to be done in each case and the experience of any one building will not necessarily be directly transferable to another.

A few of the UK's new buildings in this period have tried the approach of high thermal inertia combined with natural acclimatisation. The almost universal experience has been that despite engineers' calculations that temperature and relative humidity could be contained within BS 5454 parameters by natural means, except perhaps for very short periods in summer, in practice summer temperature has peaked at several degrees above the upper limit recommended in BS 5454 and in some cases remained there for long periods, and it has been impossible to bring it down because no means of chilling has been provided for. Unsurprisingly, where there is more than one floor of storage, the problem tends to be more marked on the upper floors. Leicestershire, London Metropolitan University Women's Library and Girton College Cambridge all eventually took one step back from a completely naturally-acclimatised building and introduced some form of chilling. Jersey[22] and Suffolk Record Office (Ipswich, featured in the previous volume)[23] were considering during this project how best to address the problem. The jury is still out in the case of the newest such building, Devon.

The ultimate in high thermal inertia − and a solution which involves no external 'building' at all − is achieved in some types of deep underground storage for archives and records. No archive service in the UK has yet adopted this solution on its own account, but it is offered commercially by a number of storage and security companies, using the now inactive parts of mines and quarries. Among these, Deepstore,[24] which occupies a substantial area underground in the Winsford salt mine in Cheshire (comprising former salt workings which are at a considerable distance from the continuing mining operation) houses archives from, among others, Cheshire Record Office and TNA. Here, the temperature and relative humidity remain constant throughout the year and can be controlled to BS 5454 parameters with only modest mechanical intervention. Tests have shown the site to be geologically and chemically stable, and an air handling system employs filters to reduce dust and other pollutants.

Natural climatisation (Photo: Deepstore)

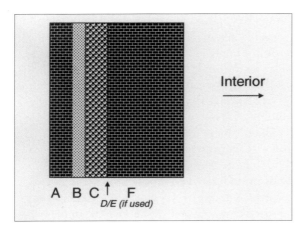

Fig. 7 *Building for high thermal inertia*
A external wall; B air gap; C insulation
(D) additional masonry (if used)
(E) second air gap (if used) F internal wall

Sample dimensions in buildings studied (mm):-

	A	B	C	D	E	F	total
Jersey	25	75	100	-	-	440	640
Norfolk	100	100	195	105	-	100	600
Staffordshire	100	50	50	-	-	200	400
York Minster Library	150	75	25	100	12.5	215	577.5
Schleswig	115	60	180	-	-	510	865

It must be stressed that many air-conditioned repositories too have found it difficult to maintain stable temperature and relative humidity within BS 5454 parameters, so the middle way, namely that of making the building's structure and fabric do most of the work whilst having the means to intervene mechanically as and when needed, has much to commend it. BS 5454 specifically recommends as follows (s.5.2.1):

> The construction should be heavy enough and air infiltration rates low enough for the temperature and relative humidity to remain stable within recommended ranges for a minimum of 24 h in the event of exceptional weather conditions or the failure of the plant.

Heavy construction

Fig. 7 shows the dimensions of walls, cavities and insulation in a sample of buildings designed to promote high thermal inertia. The normal pattern is a thick masonry exterior, a ventilated cavity or air gap, a layer of insulation and then (the thickest part) a thick

internal wall, but permutations are possible. Norfolk, for example, employs two air gaps.

Breathability/permeability

It is especially important in the case of naturally acclimatised buildings, but no less desirable in air-conditioned ones, that the fabric both externally and internally should be able to absorb and give out moisture to some degree. Equally, no excess moisture should penetrate all the way from the exterior to the interior to affect the equilibrium of the internal environment. The exact strategy for dealing with this, employing ventilated cavities and a layer of insulation, varies. Most buildings incorporate a vapour barrier to separate the internal masonry from the insulation layer. Christoffersen stresses that there should be no vapour barrier in a naturally acclimatised building,[25] but in practice, as in Jersey, one has often been employed. If the internal walls are permeable they themselves can help to regulate relative humidity by absorbing excess moisture, or by giving out moisture when the room is too dry.[26] Vapour barriers have been known to cause condensation within building fabric.

It must also be remembered when planning an archive building that many archival materials, as well as building fabrics, are to an extent hygroscopic, ie they absorb and give out moisture. This significantly affects the calculation of the controls necessary for temperature and relative humidity. More than one repository has commented that what seemed an unstable environment when monitored before occupancy quickly settled down as the archives were moved in and began to acclimatise. The opposite side of this is that large unoccupied areas of racking, which may well be a feature of new buildings in particular (since 20-years' growth may have been allowed for), will not have archives to assist in stabilisation, and may need separate control facilities, for example dehumidification, at least in the short to medium term until they are filled up.

Energy efficiency

Although archive buildings have by no means been immune from the wider concern to reduce energy consumption, there remain many whose very concept is still energy-intensive: where, for example, air-conditioning has to be left running continuously, or lighting left on throughout the working day.

Despite the existence of valuable guidance in this field,[27] a recent survey concluded that museums, libraries and archives have as yet done very little to develop energy-saving strategies, and in particular to apply the knowledge gained from their own monitoring of the storage environment to encourage energy savings.[28] Energy demands should be continually monitored and where possible reduced.

But economy in energy consumption is another of those factors which cannot be considered in isolation from the overall environmental strategy. It is inappropriate, although not unknown, to make all doors and windows airtight without ensuring adequate mechanical ventilation, to design a completely windowless repository without making some provision for internal lighting, or rigorously to conserve or recycle heat to such an extent that the ambient temperature becomes too high or the intake of fresh air insufficient. An overall plan is essential.

Ecology: a 'green' approach

As noted in the previous chapter, all building activity has an impact on the environment.[29] Responsible planners, and indeed responsible architects, must take this into account in considering a new archive building, and they are increasingly *required* to do so by European, UK national and local environment policies and building regulations. Sustainable solutions are much to be preferred. Again, useful guidance[30] is available, for example on:

- the sensitive development of sites in relation to the natural environment and the social context (impact on neighbours and the neighbourhood)[31]

- the ecological impact of the choice of particular building materials, especially non-renewables

- the add-on environmental costs of transporting materials long distances instead of using local materials and/or suppliers

- the impact on the environment of power-hungry machinery, lighting and equipment, especially air-conditioning

equipment, in terms of CO_2 emissions.[32]

Low maintenance costs

Briefs for new archive buildings understandably tend to stress the importance of minimising maintenance problems. This applies both inside and out. At the time of construction or purchase attention is so sharply focused on the one-off capital costs and whether they fall within budget that planners are often forced into trimming what should have been essentials, only to pick up the bill another year as a maintenance cost. Worse still, this can lead to the indefinite postponement of solutions. It is much more difficult to put structural and mechanical problems right once the building has been occupied and the records moved in.

These attributes of an archive building have to be taken together as a package, and not seen as individual desirables from which a selection can be made as convenient. Strong foundations are of little value if the building has a weak roof which might render it unsuitable not only on grounds of weatherproofing, but also of environment, energy consumption, maintenance costs and security. Environmental stability achieved only by massive energy consumption also falls short of the ideal.

2. OVERALL SHAPE[33]

In order to maximise the use of space there is a strong presumption in favour of square or rectangular rooms for all or most of the functions within an archive building. This offers greatest flexibility in planning the racking for both records and reference works, and the seating in search rooms, where rectangular tables offer best support to the materials being studied. It also applies in conservation workshops and reprographics facilities, to accommodate equipment and allow plenty of flat wall-space for display and mounting. Curved, acute-angled or multi-angular rooms and buildings may be more eye-catching, and can sometimes be made to work well (Westminster, York University Borthwick Institute) but experience suggests that they may result in wasted space and an inconvenient working environment.

The nature of the site and the lie of the land may not be propitious for a building that is strictly square or rectangular, but this is not essential if the individual functions inside it can be so shaped. Many different solutions have been found, some of which are illustrated in simplified form in the plans appended to the case studies below. There is no standard model.

To assist in isolating the storage areas from the influence of the external air temperature and relative humidity, some designers have opted in effect to cocoon the repository by placing other functions such as public and staff offices, or corridors/circulation space, around some or all of its outer edges, thus separating it as much as possible from the outer walls of the building.[34] This is very clear, for example, in the case of Surrey History Centre. Where this strategy – for which there are strong European precedents as noted in the previous volume[35] – is adopted, there is no less need for a high thermal inertia approach to the repository walls, and this of course adds to the cost.[36] In most cases the ambient temperature of the surrounding functions or corridors will be distinctly higher than required inside the repository, and the repository walls must act as a buffer against this influence.

In addition to the efficient use of the internal space, factors to be taken into account in planning overall shape will include:

- the cost-effective use of land

- the practicality of protecting the entire perimeter (which may argue against a low-rise building spread out over a wide area)

- the overall plan for insulating the storage areas from outside influences

- the need to provide efficient communication, whether horizontally or vertically, between related functions

- power-dependency of the whole building (eg multi-storey archive buildings cannot function without lifts)

- the need to allow for eventual extension on the site (upward extension is rarely an option given the great stresses exerted by stored archives, and is usually only possible when provided for as a contingency at the outset, as was done at Glasgow University Library)

- planning and design constraints including the impact of the building on the neighbourhood.

Glasgow University Special Collections and the City of Westminster Archives Centre have joined the House of Lords Record Office among UK record offices built in tower blocks, where special constraints apply.

Aesthetic and design considerations

Some strikingly original designs are to be found in archive buildings in this period, and a number of them have won design and architectural awards, including Leeds University's Brotherton Library extension, and Rochdale Touchstones. Extensions to existing buildings with their own powerful style, as at York Minster Library, Hereford Cathedral

Brickwork, Westminster

or Leeds University, have presented special challenges, which have been well met.

In choosing materials and ornamentation alike care must be taken to ensure that the dignity and character of the institution are appropriately reflected. The architect's natural desire to make the building look attractive should not compromise its functionality as an archive building (for example by admitting heat and light in the wrong places by too extensive use of glass, or by preventing the fabric from 'breathing' by adding impermeable external cladding for visual effect). Attention must also be paid to health and safety issues. For example, features standing proud of the main fabric should not be liable to be walked into or knocked over by staff or visitors, and should not have sharp edges or other characteristics that might cause injury.

Despite these cautionary observations, all of which arise from actual experiences reported in this period, there are many appropriate ways and means of making an archive building look attractive. Much more frequently than in the previous period, the opportunity has been taken to give distinctive character to the building, inside and out, in both the choice and the method of employment of materials, and in the sparing use of ornamentation. Plain brick exterior walls can, for example, have sections set in relief, as at Westminster, or banded in different colours for contrast, as at Essex with blue banding on ivory coloured bricks or Leicestershire with blue banding on cream and red bricks. Polished blockwork was employed in Orkney, in part to resist graffiti. Much can also be done with graphics, even in the main signage welcoming people to the building, as at Norfolk and Essex. The approach path might have ornamental paving, as at Shropshire, or the perimeter have ornamental railings as at the Cardinal Ó Fiaich Library, Armagh. An altogether more monumental approach was appropriate in the case of the British Library,[37] but appropriate 'monumentality' on a smaller scale is encountered elsewhere, as in the bronze doors at Armagh.[38] [See also appendix to this Chapter.]

Something approaching a design 'programme' has been applied in a few iconic buildings, notably Jersey, where the main public block is designed to look like an opened treasure chest, and, from the same architectural stable, the Ruskin Library at Lancaster University which has many features redolent of Ruskin himself and of Venice, and even uses the terminology of a shrine, with its 'narthex' and 'treasury'.

3. INDIVIDUAL STRUCTURAL FEATURES

With these general considerations in mind we can now turn to look at some of the particular structural features of archive buildings that have required special attention.

Walls

(a) Storage areas

In the design of the exterior of the repository, the material chosen for the outermost layer, sometimes referred to as the rain-screen, should not impede the fabric's general breathability, as discussed above, nor encourage solar gain by unduly transmitting heat to the walls behind. In practice, many different materials have been used, to suit design and aesthetic as well as practical considerations, and to blend in (or contrast) with adjacent property. They include, for example, brick, including prefabricated brick panels (National Archives of Scotland); blue-grey limestone (Cardinal Ó Fiaich Library), and terracotta tiles (Borthwick Institute York).

Walls forming part of the shell of the storage areas (which may or may not also be outer walls of the building) have to be sturdy, fire-resistant and well insulated against the influence of the external environment. Reinforced concrete or concrete blockwork are the materials most commonly used in new buildings, but of course brick, stone and some coarser, rustic building materials are not unknown, particularly in conversions.

Permeable materials used for the internal walls of a repository can assist not only in environmental control but also in the adsorption of pollutants, not least those arising from the gradual bio-deterioration of the stored materials ('off-gassing').[39] Whilst a painted internal finish is often employed – to cheer up bleak materials and enhance the working environment – micro-porous paints should preferably be used so that the fabric can still 'breathe'. One possible disadvantage of any kind of paint is that surfaces cannot easily be repainted once the records are installed. Rough, flaking wall surfaces, however, do need to be stabilised so that abrasive, usually alkaline dust does not harm the archives.[40] Non-absorbent plastic surfaces (as at Oriel and St Hilda's Oxford), have virtues such as strength and ease of cleaning, and should pose no problems in an air-conditioned repository where the equipment successfully maintains reasonable environmental equilibrium, but these surfaces might attract condensation in the event of a rapid change in the indoor environment if the equipment fails, and they bring none of the other advantages of breathable materials, so should be used with caution. In Hertfordshire two layers of perforated steel plating, with insulation in between, have been used to combine fire resistance with thermal insulation.

Pressure-relief dampers may need to be fitted to walls where an automatic gas fire-suppression system is installed. This should be determined before building.

(b) staff offices and public areas

In staff offices and public areas, a number of problems can be presented by the nature and positioning of internal walls.

- Where it is necessary to sound-proof one activity from another, any partitioning for this purpose needs to extend right up to the height of the full ceiling/internal roof and not to stop at the height of any false ceiling (or short of that).

- In a few buildings visited, certain functions which really require plenty of internal wall space (eg libraries, for book storage; conservation workshops, for equipment storage and wall-boards), have been given short measure because this was not borne in mind at the planning stage.

- Flexibility in the use of space, for example by means of sliding or de-mountable partitions, has been found very advantageous in public areas, so that entry foyers or seminar and meeting rooms can be enlarged for receptions or big meetings, or sub-divided for smaller meetings (as at Cardinal Ó Fiaich Library, Cumbria: Whitehaven, Leicestershire, York University). As already stated more comprehensive flexibility, of the kind needed to accommodate whole new functions or unexpected extra personnel,

is generally desirable, but will come with a much greater price tag which will have to be weighed against any advantages when the building is being planned.

In some smaller offices with a restricted number of staff (as at Girton College Cambridge, SOAS), and even in a few larger ones, glazed panels have been inserted in at least one of the walls connecting the public search room to adjacent staff rooms. This is not, however, recommended as the sole means of invigilation.

Floors and ceilings

Allowing for the requirements of floor-loading and fire-resistance, reinforced concrete is again the preferred material for floors in the storage areas of new buildings. Unprotected concrete screed, found particularly in converted warehouses and industrial buildings, may flake or break up with time and with the passage to and fro of trolleys. In such buildings, but also of course in new buildings, it is therefore normal to seal the floor and/or provide some form of floor covering. Care has to be taken to ensure that the materials chosen for this are inert and unlikely to decompose to the detriment of the stored records. They should also be easily swept clean. Carpeting or carpet squares are not recommended in storage areas, as they can harbour dirt and sustain insect life. In special media stores and computer rooms, where a build-up of static electricity from the wrong kind of floor covering could be harmful, special counter-measures may need to be taken such as earthing the racking, although this should be unnecessary if a suitable floor covering or sealant is used. Mezzanine flooring of open metalwork has been installed in a number of repositories. At the Royal Academy, walkways consist of a special lightweight floor made of an aluminium honeycomb within toughened glass.

In conservation and reprographics workshops flooring materials must be resistant to water and spilt chemicals. In these and any other functions throughout the building that are equipped with water services (including plant rooms), the floors should be tanked and fitted with appropriate drains.

In a number of new repositories (including the National Archives of Scotland's Thomas Thomson House and Glasgow University Library) a raised floor has been installed above the concrete base in the storage areas to carry the mobile racking on an adjustable mechanism in order to compensate for any settlement in the building. Where the storage area in new buildings is of more than one storey, troughed concrete can provide strength to the upper floors without excessive mass.

Suspended ceilings have often been introduced, to conceal the bare concrete slab or the trunking for an air-conditioning system, or (with insulation above) to reduce the volume of space to be heated, or simply to produce a storage area of more manageable size and shape. Whilst they may, on aesthetic grounds, seem an improvement on exposed raw materials, they can also conceal mishaps or design faults: rain water leaking through an air duct above the paneling, or condensation. In storage areas in particular (though in staff and public areas too) there is therefore much to be said for leaving plant and wiring exposed for easy access.

Columns and supports

Internal structural supports for the building should be kept to a minimum. They are the bane of the archivist's life. In the repository they limit the free use of storage space. In the search room, they can obstruct sight-lines for invigilation. The best designs have no such impediments, but where they are inevitable, inconvenience can be reduced or at least managed, as in Oxfordshire's converted church, if the building and shelving contractors work with the architect to plan the best use of space.

Roof

A good roof is the most critical of the frontiers between the indoor and outdoor climate, and there is clearly virtue in keeping the roof-line as simple as possible: a multiplicity of valley gutters and differential roof levels, particularly in older buildings, may lead to leaks and damp walls, and may require more assiduous maintenance, for example to prevent the build-up of organic materials.

In naturally climatised buildings (but in most others too) the outer roof, the void beneath it, and the inner roof slab below that, together play an essential role in the control of the indoor environment. They respectively keep out rain or snow, moderate the effects of the building's exposure to wind and sun, allow air to circulate freely and, with the help of appropriate insulation, buffer the rooms below so that the outdoor environmental conditions have as little impact as possible on those indoors.

Many different materials have been used for roof coverings of new archive buildings, including concrete tiles, slate, coated and/or welded stainless steel, lead, zinc, copper or aluminium, sometimes with ribbing/hipping for strength and to help channel away any water; and sometimes a combination of several of these (eg slate on steel, as at Orkney). However, it has been pointed out that lightweight materials such as aluminium and zinc might not be strong enough to stand up to heavy snow or strong wind.[41]

At Thomas Thomson House, the National Archives of Scotland used an innovative Swedish-designed roof comprising a welded stainless steel skin (172 mm) over layers of insulation.[42] Here, the parabola of the roofline is an impressive design feature, and the generous overhang of the roof beyond the outer walls, which is a feature common to many of the new buildings, further protects the walls against sun and damp. Other designs are, however, quite acceptable. At Essex and the Borthwick Institute, York, for example, the roof is contained within the outer parapet walls, with no overhang.

Flat roofs continue to be a source of worry, especially if rain water stands on them for days at a time and is not efficiently and promptly drained away, although some modern roofing materials claim to be resistant to damp, rot, puncture and tearing, as well as to fire and ultra-violet light, to be non-stretch and non-shrink, and to remain stable in a polluted environment. This requires careful evaluation by all concerned.

No matter what the roof consists of, regular and competent maintenance is critical.

In converted buildings, it may well be a case of having to live with the existing roof, but a poor roof represents a bad bargain so its condition should be thoroughly surveyed and any remedial work carried out before occupancy. As well as the inevitable leaks, problems have included weakened security through the presence of skylight windows, the use of fragile materials, and also, very commonly, heat gain/loss and condensation due to poor insulation or the use of poor quality materials.

On security grounds, roofs should not offer any unauthorised access to the building. Even at this level, inspection hatches, gallery windows, and vents large enough to admit humans should be protected by the intruder-alarm system.

The earthing for **lightning conductors** should not pass through storage areas, especially where magnetic media are stored.

Windows

Glass is fashionable as a building material, but has limitations in an archive building, particularly if the shape, size and style of windows offer any threat: to the internal environment (through solar gain, heat loss, condensation, admittance of ultra-violet light); to security (breakage and unauthorised entry); or (in the case of openable windows) through admittance of insects, dust and pollutants, and a flow of air to sustain combustion in the event of a fire.

(a) Storage areas

There are still conflicting opinions as to whether there should be any windows at all in storage areas, and if so whether they should be openable. BS 5454 (s.5.7.5) favours windowless repositories, and so does the natural climatisation model of building, where air leakage is to be kept to a minimum. The use or non-use of windows depends on a number of inter-related factors such as the orientation of the building, the presence or absence of air-conditioning, and the extent to which the records are boxed and therefore protected against exposure.[43]

Following BS 5454, many purpose-built archive buildings have completely excluded windows from their storage areas whilst in some conversions, as at Cumbria (Whitehaven), the inherited windows have been filled in. Poorly fitting windows can significantly affect a building's air-tightness and therefore the ability to control the indoor environment. They might also admit small insects. Windows more generally admit sunlight, which is unwelcome in this context.

On the other hand the admittance of some natural light, even in storage areas, offers certain advantages: potentially reducing energy demands, and providing a less claustrophobic working environment. BS 5454 acknowledges this, but recommends that where repositories

do have windows they should be small, unopenable, barred and of strengthened glass, opaque or fitted with one-way or mirrored glass if so desired, double-glazed and screened against ultra-violet light.[44] Few repositories meet all of these requirements. As long ago as 1951 it was argued that 'no repository should be so constructed that ventilation by doors and windows could not be used'.[45] This still deserves to be carefully pondered. Small, openable windows with blinds to keep out light are fitted at Glasgow University Library Special Collections. Not only would these allow additional ventilation if necessary, but they are a means of access for maintenance of the external fabric at the top of this multi-storey building.

(b) Other parts of the building

Elsewhere in the building the general concern is to minimise direct sunlight on records wherever they are being consulted or worked on. This can be achieved by orientation or other design features, or by screens, blinds and/or ultra-violet filters which may be integral to the glass (costly but effective and durable) or applied as a film to the surface (cheaper but needing periodic renewal). Several new buildings, including the Borthwick Institute York, Essex Record Office and Girton College Cambridge (see case study) have structural baffles on the exterior of the reading room windows, or windows themselves angled in such a way as to deflect sunlight away from readers' tables. Berkshire and Norfolk record offices are among those with automated slatted blinds for use as necessary.

In areas set aside for reading microforms or consulting computer screens, subdued light is helpful. Some have used completely windowless rooms for these purposes; some have used low-level lighting controllable for example by dimmer switches (National Library of Wales). Draught as well as light and security needs to be reckoned with when considering openable windows in public areas and offices.

Natural light is important to conservators, but direct sunlight is not welcome in workshops and exhibition areas. So, for conservation (in the UK) a north or east light is best and natural light generally preferable to artificial. The orientation of many new buildings, and the placing of functions within them should normally take this into account, but this has not always happened, and it may not be an option in a converted building.

Except in limited contexts such as plant rooms and reprographics workshops, windowless rooms make for an inconvenient working environment. The quality of life is unquestionably enhanced by windows offering a visual point of reference outside the room, still more if the view is inspiring. Offices with no outlook, especially where they are tucked away in the centre of a building far from natural light, or (worse still) wholly enclosed with no windows, are depressing. Light can sometimes be shared, and a more open, less claustrophobic effect created, by the judicious use of glazed panels instead of solid walls, as between the reception area and the reading room at Leeds University.

Doors

For security reasons, in an archive building the number of entries and exits for public, staff and records is best kept to the minimum necessary for compliance with fire and safety regulations on the one hand and efficient management on the other. Certain converted buildings have been found to be over-endowed with doors, some of which have had to be blocked up or protected round the clock by the intruder-alarm system. In the best designed purpose-built buildings the number of doors openable from the outside is deliberately restricted, indeed preferably kept to a single one, and there is no direct access from the outdoors into a storage area. Conversely

fire-escape doors opening directly from a strongroom to the outside are made openable only from the inside.

On security and environmental grounds, outer doors ought to be weatherproof, air-tight, strong and fire-resistant. Conventional domestic or office doors inherited in buildings for conversion have not been found adequate, and here and there even purpose-built doors have not proved equal to the prevailing weather conditions. Further problems occur if there are gaps below or around the doors, through which dust, insects, or the elements – including of course un-treated air – can enter the repository. In the case of glazed doors or panels, including also extensively glazed external walkways and linking corridors, special attention should be given to the strength of the materials. Additional defences can of course be provided, as at Hertfordshire where the entrance lobby to the new (detached) strongroom building is fitted with a steel roller shutter which is lowered when the building is unoccupied.

In order to conform with security and fire-resistance requirements internal doors forming part of the shell of the storage areas are normally of solid metal or thick wood (or a combination of the two). The width of all internal doors has to allow for the transit of trolleys etc loaded with records, and the movement of individual large documents or furniture around the building. For ease of production, the number of doors to be negotiated between the storage area and the search room should be minimised.

Appendix to Chapter 4

Commissioned works of art

A welcome, and growing, trend in this period has been the commissioning of works of art to humanise the building and assert its wider links with the culture of the community. Examples include the local history tapestry in the foyer of the Surrey Record Centre, stained or engraved glass at Jersey, Shropshire, Surrey and Westminster, the carved stone inscription on the new block at Churchill Archive Centre Cambridge, children's wood pulp art inspired by local scenes at Cumbria Record Office,

Turkish rug, Girton.

Whitehaven, a specially commissioned Turkish rug at Girton College Cambridge, and many paintings and three-dimensional works.
Good design can of course be applied to the furniture as well, particularly chairs and tables in the public areas. At the Royal Academy of Arts' new archives, as one would expect, high standards of craftsmanship and design were applied to everything from leather-topped work benches to colour-matched doors and even telephones).

Pebble art, Shropshire

Logo art, Norfolk

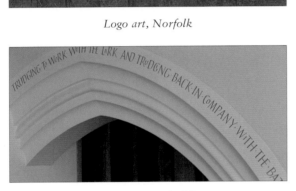

Inscription, Oxfordshire

Commissioned art, Norfolk

Children's art, Whitehaven

Chapter 5

SECURITY[1]

(BS 5454:2000 ss.4.3, 5.7)

'Security', in the sense of the term now usually applied in manuals for archives, libraries and museums, is the protection of the holdings against all potential causes of stress, damage or loss. This is of the very essence of a 'repository'. The separate treatment given in BS 5454, and in the chapters of this book, to the choice of site and materials, the planning and design of the building, and protection against fire and adverse environmental conditions, is for convenience only. All of these will have to be taken into account when formulating an overall security strategy for the building, and none can be considered in isolation without weakening the strategy. The present chapter, therefore, although confined mainly to protection against deliberate criminal acts, should be seen in that wider context.

The incidence of vandalism and theft

No comprehensive figures have been compiled on the incidence of vandalism and theft in the United Kingdom's record repositories, but (as was also true at the time of the previous volume) enough individual cases have been reported to demonstrate a need for vigilance. Repositories are naturally reluctant to discuss their vulnerability or reveal the precise measures taken to prevent incidents. There is a strong case for withholding full details of the defences, including the exact location of detection and alarm devices, except perhaps in the public areas, where their visibility might prove a deterrent. Those repositories which allow public visits behind the scenes should take this into account.

Vandalism, and other behaviour which might (perhaps unthinkingly and without any malice aforethought) put the archives at risk, remains a more widespread problem than theft. In the case of archive buildings, vandalism appears to be random and opportunistic, and not targeted on archives for their own sake. What attracts is probably the opportunity presented by a building's location, features, structure and materials to satisfy the vandal's destructive urges: shrubs which can be hacked down, large areas of uninterrupted wall ideal for graffiti, windows that make good targets for projectiles, grounds ample enough for ball-games out of hours, flat roofs on which pranks can be performed (including one reported case of a hidden part of a roof being equipped with cushions and used as a trysting place by the local youth!), and so on. The fear is that vandalism or even relatively innocent pranks might, simply because of the opportunity offered, lead into crime such as breaking and entry, arson, or the theft of lead or other roofing materials.

Attacks by disaffected members of staff do not seem to be a problem for archive buildings in the UK. But in view of the high percentage of general fires attributed to arson, and their incidence in certain types of building, including notably schools, those contemplating converting a building for archival use will wish to take appropriate precautions against anyone who might have had a grudge against a previous occupier and who might not be aware of the building's change of use.

On the whole, archive buildings are not promising places for random or speculative thefts involving break-ins. Few other than initiates – staff and readers – have any idea what they contain, let alone its value. There are exceptions, for example in the case of national repositories and university libraries, where individual items and their value might be well publicised.

Archive strongrooms are doubly unpromising because even a thief who knows roughly what they contain will need to penetrate certain physical barriers and unknown degrees of security to reach them, and then need to know what is where, among anonymous-looking storage boxes. Any overview of security strategy must, however, take account of the risk of theft by a member of the staff, who will be better informed.

No repository in the UK has reported any break-in in this period that was motivated

by the desire to steal records. The thieves, or
rather would-be thieves, since most of them
have been caught or scared off by the sounding
of intruder alarms, have mostly been after cash
or movables such as computer and video equipment. Attention needs to be paid to this risk
when planning and protecting the public and
staff accommodation of any archive building.

Unfortunately, however, thefts *without*
break-ins have proved all too easy during
normal opening hours! Making the records
available for public inspection might be thought
almost as central as security to the concept
of the record repository. But this more than
any other single factor is what exposes them
to risk. When they are removed from their
safe storage for inspection in the search room
their nature and content, perhaps known only
dimly up to that point from a description in
a finding-aid, become apparent to the reader.
For a while the baton of custodial trust
changes hands. It is the price most owners and
custodians of archives willingly pay to share
our written heritage as widely as possible. Very
occasionally that trust is broken.

Most known thefts of records in the UK
seem to have been motivated by a desire to
possess particular kinds of documents – or
parts of documents, such as maps, stamps,
autographs and photographs – either to add
to a private collection or to make money by
selling them. A few breaches of security have
hit national headlines in the period, including
two widely-reported cases which affected a
considerable number of archives, where thieves
went about the country respectively seeking
out fine maps and photographs of children.
Unscrupulous readers might also wish to
tamper with evidence by removing or defacing
documents or conversely, as in a recent case
at The National Archives, by adding forged
documents to a real record.

The costs of tighter security can be offset
against those of the staff time that would
have to be spent in unscrambling the problems
arising from stolen (and, just as pertinent,
subsequently repatriated) records, and against
the lost good will of owners.

How much security?

Manuals on security make the point that
before embarking on specific security measures
custodians should assess the nature and degree
of the risks involved, so that the defences may

be proportionate. This applies on two levels: to
the holdings themselves, where common sense
might dictate that the most precious objects
should receive the greatest degree of protection;
but also to the various areas and functions of
the building, some of which might by nature be
less vulnerable or offer less potential reward to
intruders.

As far as the holdings are concerned,
archives can be viewed differently from museum
exhibits. Some documents or collections are
of such importance or sensitivity, or of such
high monetary value, as to require special
security measures. For this reason a number of
repositories, for example the British Library
and a number of university special collections,
have set aside high security or 'safe' rooms,
caged areas, or other zones to which access
is controlled more strictly than to the rest of
the repository. Rare reference books may need
similar protection. But this must not lead to the
thought that material of less value can be left
to look after itself. Each item irrespective of its
value is unique and irreplaceable. None that
are worthy of permanent preservation should
be left at risk as a result of weak security
provision.

As for the buildings, greater round-the-clock
security should apply to any rooms or areas in
which records are housed than, for example,
to general staff offices and public areas. And
indeed this assumption underlies the planning
and structure of most repositories. It is not
necessary to set up defences worthy of Fort
Knox for the contents of a cleaner's store
cupboard. But on the other hand if intrusion
into the public or staff areas is made unduly
easy because security is pitched too low, there
is no knowing what damage may follow, even
to the records.

A proper security strategy, actively reviewed
from time to time, is desirable in every
archive building. Some security measures are
inexpensive and can be achieved by relatively
low-tech means. Indeed, there is much to be
said for simplicity. As one commentator puts it:

> The archivist who relies on common sense
> and ingenuity will have a more secure
> repository than the archivist who depends
> solely on sophisticated security equipment.[2]

Some of the essential yet affordable
security measures are more to do with good
management than with good buildings:

control of public admissions; staff selection procedures, staff complement, duties, training and discipline; control of acquisitions and the means of issue and retrieval of documents; control of keys, and so on.[3] The general upgrading of admissions requirements/ readers' tickets has continued. Other security measures vary from place to place but include restrictions on the number of items which may be handed to a reader at a time, stamping or marking the documents, or weighing them as they enter and leave the search room. These measures ought to be cost-effective since they focus specifically on the area of highest risk: the public search room. No security measures, however, should be thought invincible: an experienced and determined thief can find a way through most defences.

The perimeter

Good security begins at the perimeter, whether that is interpreted as the boundary of the grounds or the outer wall of the archive building. BS 5454:2000 (s.4.3) recommends that a record repository should be demarcated from surrounding land by a perimeter fence. A physical barrier of this kind, if sufficiently high and robust, kept locked outside office hours, and not so opaque as to prevent anyone outside seeing what is taking place behind it, may deter criminals.[4] That depends on the neighbourhood, and the likelihood of anyone being detected scaling the fence. It may be both feasible and desirable on a new site to erect a fence. And some converted buildings, especially schools, come provided with one. But it has often proved impractical, for example in the context of a historic site, a building on a campus of other unfenced properties, a building directly beside (say) a street or a canal-side path, or where planners insist on an open-plan approach. In such cases the 'perimeter' has to be differently defined. But it is worth remembering that the absence of a defined perimeter has been known to increase exposure of the fabric to graffiti and vandalism.

Whether or not a fence is provided, it is appropriate to examine the building and its surroundings through the eyes of a potential vandal or thief, with the help of the local police Crime Prevention Officer or, if appropriate, the museums' National Security Adviser.[5] Will all of the exterior be visible from surrounding properties or streets? If some will be concealed from view, does that include possible points of entry, which will therefore require special protection? Is there anything in the structure of the building or in the lie of the surrounding land or the landscaping which might offer cover or facilitate unauthorised access (eg sloping land offering easy access to a low roof; trees or shrubs concealing doors or windows, or offering a means of scaling walls)?

Security lighting and external CCTV

Security lighting of the perimeter has been installed as an additional or alternative deterrent by a number of repositories: built into the outer walls or in the form of flood-lighting from a distance. Lighting on the outer wall of the building itself should preferably be fitted structurally, in such as way that bulbs and other parts of the fitting cannot easily be damaged or tampered with.[6] Some have also installed exterior closed-circuit television, usually with video recording facilities but in at least one case using only dummy equipment, as a deterrent. The grounds of one repository are protected by a security cordon of infra-red beams linked to the alarm system.

Intruder alarms

Whilst it is possible to equip the fence, or any open area surrounding the building, with intruder-detectors, in practice most repositories have tended to concentrate their limited budgets on detecting either the actual penetration of the shell by the breaking of doors or windows, or the resulting invasion of internal space.

Access points to the building, other than the main public entrance, require entry controls or intruder-alarms which operate round the clock. This is especially true of any external doors, loading bays etc which are not permanently visible to a member of staff, and fire doors or other exits intended for use only in a emergency. It is not necessary for a new building to be so designed that public routes, whether for general transit, access to WCs or even fire-escapes, pass through restricted areas. Occasionally in the case of adapted buildings this is unavoidable, and then additional security measures are necessary.

BS 5454:2000 (s.5.7.2) recommends that an intruder-alarm system be provided in accordance with BS 4737-1. The inspecting authorities further recommend that the alarm be linked to a security agency, a practice now widely adopted. An alarm bell alone, although it may drive off intruders, is not a satisfactory substitute. Some favour an alarm which alerts the security authorities without ringing a bell on the site, thus perhaps improving the chances of catching the intruder red-handed; the effectiveness of such a strategy depends very much on the speed of response to any call.

The various kinds of alarm available are described in detail in a number of manuals[7] but the technology is continually changing. The choice of system, or combination of systems suited to local needs, is best discussed with the Crime Prevention Officer rather than directly with the alarm manufacturers, who may be concerned to sell a particular product. Alarms fall into two broad categories: those which detect the penetration of the building's shell and those which detect movement, sound or heat within. In repositories housing audio-visual and magnetic media, special care has to be taken to ensure that beams or fields from the alarm equipment cannot pose any threat to the integrity of the stored media.

Both security- and fire-alarms can be extremely sensitive instruments. False security alerts have been caused in archive buildings by vibrations, noise or lights (even outside the building), lightning, air turbulence, twigs being blown against a window, a poster falling off a wall, spiders, flies and insects, and even by the movement of water in fall-pipes. Careful location and angling of the detectors can help, and to minimise the number of false alarms it may be advisable to increase the number and type of sensors that have to be activated before the alarm sounds.

Locks

BS 5454:2000 (s.5.7.6) recommends that all doors be fitted with locks conforming to BS 3621.[8] Locks fitted to strongroom doors should (for the safety of staff) in addition be openable from the inside without a key. Attention must also be paid to the control of keys, and to the avoidance of exposed external door-hinges and pins, which could be removed. In the event of any doors being electronically controlled, the disaster plan must take account not only of security but also of the means of access in the event of a power failure.

Controlling public access

A clearly signed public entrance, preferably on the same level of the building as the search room, is a useful defence against a visitor wandering in through any other door (although no other points of entry should be left unlocked). Where staffing is stretched, or the search room is some distance from the front door, a number of repositories control entry to the foyer/entrance lobby by means of an entry-phone (eg Cumbria: Whitehaven; Warwickshire), although this can seem somewhat off-putting to a first-time user. Where, alternatively, the outer door is left unlocked during office hours, admittance should normally be either to a staffed reception area or to a hall or corridor from which the onward public route is unambiguous. In a few buildings where the staff reception desk (or even the search room invigilation desk) is staffed by a single person and is rather isolated from the nearest other member of staff, panic buttons have been provided to allow staff to summon help from colleagues in an emergency.

Many repositories now use combination locks or electronic or magnetic swipe cards (issued to designated holders only, and often with varying levels of restriction) to control access to areas of the building from which the public is excluded. The main entrance can be a weak spot in the security of buildings converted from other uses if, as is often the case, it is a confluence of corridors from the different parts of the building, or of stairs or lift(s) giving access to all floors. Where the use of the same lift for access to public and staff-only areas is unavoidable, a security key control system should be fitted in order to confine public access to authorised areas. Directional signs, inside as well as out, have a vital part to play, but unless the entrance is permanently staffed and it can be guaranteed that the staff's attention will not be diverted, physical barriers such as lockable doors and partitions will be needed to channel the public in the right direction.

There is now usually, as a matter of course, provision for the deposit of readers' coats and bags in self-service lockers provided for the purpose. These should not be situated within the search room itself unless they are on the outside of a security check-point which readers have to pass before reclaiming their bags.

Search room

The public search room should be regarded as a high security area which ideally has only one point of public entry/exit (apart from any alarmed emergency exits), on which staff attention can be properly concentrated. Entry, and more particularly exit, might for example be controlled by a security gate or turnstile operated by a member of staff (as at the National Library of Wales and TNA). In the largest repositories, where a single door may be impractical, special care has to be taken over securing the whole public area.

The number and location of invigilation points in a search room naturally vary according to the size and shape of the room. It has been observed that to some extent readers informally 'invigilate' one another,[9] although this should not be relied on as the only strategy. In a number of buildings visited (Essex, National Library of Wales, Cardinal Ó Fiaich Library), staff offices with windows on to the search area are arranged down one side of the room for additional security. Where there is a free choice in the design, a room of simple square or rectangular shape, but not too long and narrow, is preferable to one of irregular shape with alcoves or blind corners which make for difficult invigilation. The best designed search rooms have no pillars or columns to impede sight-lines, or at least have readers' tables and chairs so placed that they are not hidden from view. The height and positioning of free-standing bookcases, filing cabinets and other furniture, especially where used to differentiate functions such as reference or microfilm areas, should not block sight-lines.

There is no adequate substitute for human invigilation. All other security systems, such as recording closed-circuit television (now very widely used), convex mirrors and magnetic or radio-frequency strips on reference books, have to be regarded as only a second tier of defence. If carefully designed, small and medium-sized search rooms may be effectively invigilated from a single staff point. But with the increasing trend among larger services to assign separate though linked areas for consultation of finding-aids, local studies material, microfilm and original records respectively, even a single point sometimes has to be staffed by more than one person. A raised dais or platform, as at Denbighshire, can give a better view, but care should be taken that the height of any furniture and fittings does not impede access by disabled people.

No opportunity should be given to a thief to leave the search room, even temporarily, other than by the main entrance. Lifts and stairs should therefore not open directly into the search room – still a problem in converted buildings, and even in some libraries – nor should there be other public rooms such as WCs immediately accessible from the search room, unless they are beyond a security check point. Thieves have been known to take records into a WC or wash room and hide them about their person or drop them out of a window.

Other public areas

Although generally less sensitive than the search room, all the other public areas of the building require some security protection. The most important general principle is that the public, including contractors and anyone else not on the repository staff, should not be able to wander unaccompanied into any of the non-public areas, either accidentally or by design. Specific monitoring or invigilation is needed in any display area, if original records are exhibited, and in the latter case security should be no less stringent than in the search room.

Some security problems reported in this period

- A number of break-ins and thefts of equipment, as reported above.

- A building with satisfactory alarms on its doors was broken into through a skylight window which, owing to an oversight, had not been alarmed.

- Entry to one building was gained via an adjacent property and then along the roof to a skylight window which was kept unlocked for use as a fire escape. (The alarm was sounded as soon as the entry was made and the intruder fled).

- In the absence of a secure perimeter, a tramp set up his bed under a sheltered canopy outside one archive building at night and lit a fire in a corner, against the outer wall. (This triggered the building's fire alarm and caused only minor damage).

Chapter 6

FIRE PREVENTION[1]

(BS 5454:2000, s.5.3 and 6)

Fire prevention has already been alluded to in discussing the choice of site and building materials. This chapter is concerned more particularly with non-structural aspects of the subject.

Key developments in this period

The period under review has seen a number of important developments with respect to fire, and fire prevention, in archives:

- Alas, the situation is not as theoretical as it was at the time of the previous volume: there have been a number of real and damaging fires.

- One important consequence is that more thought has been given to fire prevention, detection, alarm and control as applied to archives.

- BS 5454:2000 for the first time accepted the use of water in automatic fire suppression systems for archives.

- With the phasing out of halons as fire suppressants, new gaseous agents have been developed, some of which are particularly suitable for use in archives.

Actual fires

The worst fire in a UK archive building was that at Norwich Central Library in 1994, originating in electrical equipment.[2] The County Record Office was housed in the basement. During the fire-fighting the archives suffered significant water damage – fortunately most of it reparable – but they were soundly protected against fire. The building itself, however, was rendered unusable. The record office had to be evacuated, initially to temporary accommodation elsewhere in the city, pending construction of the new Norfolk Archives Centre. East Sussex experienced a near miss, also in 1994, when another part of a building used as an archives out-store was set alight by an arsonist. A fire which caused major damage and loss in a modern records store in

Northamptonshire in 1996 was started by a workman's unattended blow-lamp. Fire also destroyed Ramsgate Library in 2004, although fortunately the archives once held there had been removed.[3]

The nature of the risk

Archives themselves are not a fire risk, with the exception of cellulose nitrate film which requires special storage conditions because it can ignite spontaneously (BS 5454:2000 s.11.4.2). On the other hand, virtually all archival media are combustible; indeed they will often represent the highest fire 'load' in the building in which they are housed. So they must be isolated from the risk, whether that arises from deliberate or negligent human action or the malfunctioning of machinery or equipment.

Managing the risk (BS 5454:2000 s.6)

When planning a fire prevention strategy, the advice of the local fire authority should be sought. But it should also be borne in mind that the first responsibility of the fire services is to protect against loss of life, and other harm to humans. For archives, there are other specific issues to take into account. This will have an influence on, for example, the means of access to the building in the event of an emergency, the routes of fire escapes, and the choice of fire suppressant(s). Archivists should apprise the brigade of the special nature of the building's contents and the need to use the minimum amount of water in any emergency.

Most fires are preventable, but preparedness is proportionate to the time spent in formulating a **risk management strategy**, which will include predicting how a fire might start, and then putting appropriate counter-measures in place. The risks can be minimised by the choice of a suitable site; by appropriate building design, construction and fitting-out, including the use of fire-resistant materials and finishes; by care in the selection, installation and above all the regular maintenance of plant and services; by the provision of equipment for fire detection and suppression; by general attention to security; and by good housekeeping and management.

At the planning stage the most important precaution is the prudent siting of any functions or stores identified as potential sources of fire: plant for heating and air-conditioning; the mains electrical supply; facilities such as kitchens or canteens; and areas in which flammable substances including paint and cleaning materials, and reprographics and conservation materials, are to be stored. Some of these are in any case subject to the Control of Substances Hazardous to Health regulations. Most repositories have taken heed of the recommendation (BS 5454:2000 s.6.4.5) that it should be possible to isolate electrical equipment out of office hours. Some power is needed even then, to serve air-conditioning equipment and the detection and alarm systems.

Detection and alarm (BS 5454 s.6.6)

New repositories now almost invariably have alarms linked to the fire brigade, either directly or through an intermediate agent such as a security firm. Whether the building is staffed or deserted, whether it is protected by an automatic fire-suppression system or not, a reliable means of detecting a fire and actively raising the alarm is indispensable. An alarm that sounds only on the premises is not sufficient, except perhaps where the building is staffed and patrolled throughout the 24 hours every day of the year.

Detectors

Several kinds of detector are available, designed for differing circumstances. They detect respectively heat, or rapid changes in temperature; smoke; or flame. They must not be obstructed by shelving or other furniture or equipment, and since their optimum siting varies with the height of the room, the pitch or angle of the ceiling and, in storage areas, the amount of vertical space above the racking,[4] equipment inherited from a previous tenant in a converted building cannot be assumed to be effective in the new context without experiment. The siting of detectors requires skilled judgement. For example they should not be fitted in a place where rising heat from a heating system can deflect any smoke away,

nor in such a relation to air-conditioning vents etc that cooler air blows past them, preventing them detecting abnormal rises in temperature perhaps just a few feet away.[5]

As a safeguard against false alarms (which can be caused by a number of factors such as dust rising during building works, or heavy vapours rising from a conservation work-bench) it may be worth installing two different kinds of detector, for example smoke and ionisation detectors. For archives, smoke detectors are preferable to heat detectors because paper can smoulder before igniting. Heat detectors alone failed to detect the Norwich fire until it was too late, and in tests they also failed to trigger a water mist system before a fire had taken hold.[6]

Greatest assurance is offered by an aspir-ating detection system such as VESDA® (Very Early Smoke Detection Apparatus)[7] which continuously samples the air throughout the room (rather than at a few fixed points as with most other detectors) and notes any abnor-malities in order to detect a fire in the incipient phase: that is, before there is a flame. Systems of this kind are now being widely installed in archive buildings throughout the UK.

Fire suppression[8]

NOTE: *Information given below is based on the experience of British repositories in the period, and on published manuals and guidance, and should not be quoted as a primary authority. The advice of the local Fire Officer should always be taken.*

Fires are extinguished principally by sharply reducing the temperature of the burning material, by cutting off or reducing the oxygen supply, or by interfering chemically with the process of combustion. There is no single solution that can be applied in every context, so the needs of the particular building must be carefully evaluated. Much depends on the size and nature of the areas to be protected: notably, the number and size of rooms and the extent of other compartmentation.

The best all-round protection comes from fully automatic fire-suppression systems. These may be unnecessary where an archive building is staffed round the clock and there can be rapid human response to an alarm, or where the building is situated very close to a fire station (but, as noted above, this can change). However, where no automatic system is installed all other precautions have to be redoubled, and a detection and alarm system linked to the brigade or to a monitoring firm will assume special importance.

Water sprinklers

The 2000 edition of BS 5454 for the first time accepted water sprinklers, on a par with gas systems, as a satisfactory means of fire suppression in archives. This followed growing international research[9] and experience of their use, concluding that there was a very low risk of sprinkler head failure and only minor incidents of accidental discharge. The National Archives of Australia 'will not store records regardless of their value in any building that does not have sprinklers'.[10]

The rationale for their use is straightforward. Water quickly and safely suppresses a fire in most kinds of archival documents. Of course the archives will get wet if sprinklers are used, but this is also the case in any fire where the brigade use water hoses. In the case of sprinklers, water will be discharged only around the seat of the fire. Water damage can be limited by boxing the archives. Wet or damp archives can often be rescued and repaired; there is much less hope for them if they get burnt. Water poses no harm to the environment and is available cheaply. It may be the only realistic agent for an automated suppression system that has to cover storage space of large volume, where a gas system could be inoperable or too expensive.

Sprinklers have been installed at, among other places, the National Archives of Scotland (Thomas Thomson House), the National Library of Scotland following a very thorough fire risk assessment of the whole of the original building on George IV Bridge, Edinburgh,[11] London Metropolitan Archives and the British Library. In a number of other repositories including Devon Record Office and the National Library of Wales a gas suppression system is used in the archive storage areas but water sprinklers elsewhere in the building.[12]

Sprinklers cannot be contemplated unless there is a guaranteed and sufficient supply of water, either direct from the mains or from tanks installed for this purpose. For large repositories such as those mentioned above, the tanks required are of formidable size, and careful planning was needed to identify space to house them.

Several different sprinkler systems are available, the main choice being between wet- and dry-pipe systems. As the name implies, in a wet-pipe system water is in the pipes all the time, waiting to be triggered via the sprinkler head in an emergency. The advantage is that it is ready for immediate action if needed. The main risks are of leakage or accidental discharge, but these should not be a problem in a properly maintained system, and no significant incidents have been reported in practice. In a dry-pipe system the pipes are empty or filled with a gas until activated, when water rushes in. There is a fractional delay in activation compared with a wet-pipe system. There can still be a risk of leakage, for example from condensation forming in the pipework. In both systems it is an advantage for the pipes to be made of non-corrosible material such as strong plastic or stainless steel (although this will push up the cost of installation).

Water is not normally discharged until two separate sensors confirm that there is an emergency and trigger the system. Even then, it is discharged only from those sprinkler heads in the immediate vicinity of the fire. One sprinkler head can have an impressive range, and in many cases a single activated head will be sufficient to put out a fire. To be effective, sprinklers require a specified minimum clearance above the height of the racking, usually of at least half a metre. This should be checked in advance with the supplier.

Some difficulty arises over sprinklers in storage areas fitted with mobile racking, because the water has to be able to penetrate to the seat of any fire. Some electronic racking can be programmed to set the units apart out of hours to enable sprinklers to operate effectively if needed. At the National Archives of Scotland the mobile shelving units are kept 30 mm apart by means of rubber stops.

Whether or not a sprinkler system is used, provision should be made – though this has not always been remembered – for the evacuation of any water and smoke accumulating in the repository in the event of a fire. This is particularly important in basements (although, as the Norwich case showed, basement accommodation can sometimes have its advantages in a fire).

Water mist systems[13]

Water mist systems, which again come in several varieties mainly requiring a choice between high- and low-pressure operation, have been installed in a number of historic libraries elsewhere in Europe, and in some business archives and record stores in the UK including London Transport and Railtrack, but not in any public archive repositories visited in the course of this survey. They work by releasing droplets of water which vaporise and quickly reduce the volume of space available for oxygen that could sustain a fire. The systems are more effective in large areas of well spaced racking than in mobile racking, and more effective in high- than in low- intensity fires. In tests conducted by the National Archives of Scotland in the course of planning for the next phase of Thomas Thomson House it was established that mist systems required pipes of significantly smaller gauge than sprinkler systems (an aesthetic as well as a practical advantage), that they used only about 10% as much water so required much less water to be stored, and that they swiftly and effectively suppressed a fire provided that there was rapid detection and activation of the system. Documents in boxes suffered no damage.[14] As with all water-based systems the water supply and the pipework must be clean to ensure that the heads do not become blocked.

Gas

Under the Montreal Protocol, the use of halons in fire fighting was phased out in the UK in the early 1990s on environmental grounds, because of their ozone-depleting property. Decommissioning of halon had to be completed by the end of 1993. A number of permitted replacement gases have been developed which do not have ozone-depleting properties. All are effective in fire suppression, which is the most important consideration. But reservations attach to some gaseous agents on account of either their wider effects on the environment or the potential harm that might be done specifically to archives as a result of by-products in the event of a fire.

Most UK archives with automated gas suppression systems have opted for **Inergen®** or **Argonite®**, two products which combine the inert gas argon with one or more other gases (nitrogen and carbon dioxide) that are already prevalent in the atmosphere. There are

Norfolk fire protection

no known harmful by-products. These systems work best in a room of limited size with good airtightness, as they aim to flood the space with gas to reduce the amount of oxygen to below the level (around 12-14%) at which a fire can be sustained. More gas cylinders are required than was the case for halon, and this needs to be taken into account at both planning and installation stages. On the other hand, as a cost-saving measure where a number of separate rooms are involved and the likelihood of fire breaking out in all the rooms simultaneously is small, some repositories have installed pipes throughout but with only enough gas to serve one space in the event of any incident.

These gases are normally released under considerable pressure, which can quickly disperse loose papers. In converted older buildings the fabric will need to be carefully surveyed to ensure that it will withstand the pressure. In buildings purpose-designed to have this form of fire-suppression system special pressure-release mechanisms will be needed, for example in the form of louvres in the outer walls. A lower pressure system is available.

Argon on its own was in use in one repository visited for this study.

FM200® is another gas in use in a number of repositories. Its manufacturers have published an open and honest assessment of its properties[15] which makes clear that it is a greenhouse gas and that one of its by-products, hydrogen fluoride is acidic (as was the case with halons). This might suggest it is less environmentally friendly than the inert gases

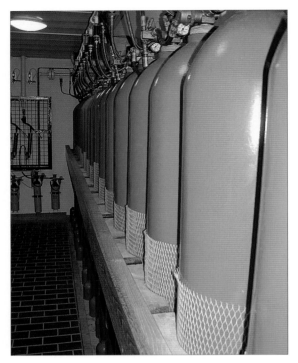

Argonite bottles, Hereford Cathedral

above, but if the fire is suppressed quickly and the storage environment thereafter promptly cleaned and the atmosphere refreshed it does not seem likely that there will be any damaging long-term exposure of archives to HF.

Carbon dioxide is still used in a few archive repositories but is no longer the system of choice in a new purpose-designed building, mainly on health and safety grounds. It is not known to damage records or equipment, but as it relies for its effectiveness on replacing the available oxygen, human exposure to the gas at this concentration could result in suffocation. To avoid any such problem, the system must therefore be well regulated, with an alarm sounding to warn staff of the gas being deployed.

Reduced oxygen solutions

As this study was in the press a number of national institutions were actively considering a new solution to fire prevention which has been deployed overseas but not yet in archive buildings in the UK. Under this system, nitrogen is fed into the storage environment to keep the volume of oxygen permanently below that at which combustion is sustainable. More research and practical experience is needed before it could be said that this technique is an obvious choice for archive storage, and it has

some obvious drawbacks. It is energy intensive to use, and as it requires a very high degree of airtightness in the fabric of the building it can probably best be considered only where there is going to be very limited access to the stored materials.

At the English Heritage National Monuments Record repository, which specialises in the storage of photographic materials, the air intake system can be reversed in the event of any fire, to suck out the air and stifle the fire.

Fire hydrants and hand-held extinguishers (BS 5454:2000 s.6.7.4-6)

Whether or not an automatic suppression system is provided, manual means of extinguishing small fires are required, and again the advice of the Fire Officer should be sought. Hand-held extinguishers are usually wall-mounted in order not to obstruct corridors and circulation space. Public areas and corridors are most effectively protected by water-based fire-extinguishers (for small fires) or water hoses (for larger fires). Dedicated fire hydrants may be required by law, especially in high-rise buildings. At the City of Westminster Archives Centre, for example, these are provided on each landing of the multi-storey building. Water is effective for the commonest fires, involving paper and wood, but must not be used on electrical fires or those involving flammable liquids and chemicals.

Record storage areas and electrical equipment are best protected with carbon dioxide fire extinguishers. Dry powder extinguishers may be used in the case of electrical fires and those involving flammable liquids and gases, and are generally safe for use with paper and parchment but not newer media.[16]

Fire blankets still have a role in certain parts of the building, particularly workshops and kitchens where naked flames may be expected.

Security, housekeeping and management

Other aspects of fire prevention which relate more particularly to good housekeeping and management are not a principal concern of this volume but may be briefly listed. A number of them are covered in BS 5454 and in the chapter above on security. In particular:

- There should be no unauthorised admittance.

- A No-Smoking rule should be strictly enforced. Visitors and contractors should be made aware of the rule.

- No form of heating which includes a naked flame or element should be used in repository or offices.

- Combustible materials should not be placed on or beside heating services, in or adjacent to boiler rooms, or beside fuse boxes, mains switches or electrical equipment.

- Combustible materials including waste paper etc but also the records themselves should not be left on floors or in other places where they might become liable to combustion in the event of carelessness, eg in the discarding of an illicit lighted cigarette.

- Flammable liquids should be stored away from sources of heat, in air-tight containers. Some may be liable to ignite spontaneously without exposure to any naked flame or spark.

- Regular inspections of the repository should be undertaken by the professional staff to ensure that the fire regulations are being observed.

- All electrical equipment should be regularly tested.

- Regular fire drills should be held and good relations maintained with the fire brigade which should be given standing instructions on the nature and location of the building.

- There should be a disaster recovery plan.

Fire-escapes

No new archive building should be so designed that an area used for the storage of archives also serves as a general fire-escape route (other than for staff working there at the time of the fire). Where, in a conversion or extension, this is unavoidable, additional security measures should be taken, including the use of alarms to detect the unauthorised opening of strong-room and fire-escape doors. Fire-escape doors from the storage areas are, however, often necessary for staff use, and are best designed to open only from the inside.

Vigilance is necessary: some problems reported in this period

- A gas system had to be replaced after the end of its natural life when the new fittings were all different and the old installation could not be re-used.

- In a real fire in a cold store for photographs, smoke stayed low in the room because of the low temperature, and was not detected by smoke detectors fitted to the ceiling.

- The gas in 8 out of a total of 20 cylinders in one repository was discharged in error before the system was fully commissioned, owing to a false alarm.

- In another case gas seeped out of the storage cylinders because they were incorrectly fitted, with a valve not tightened.

- In a converted building with sprinklers already fitted it was found that because the ignition temperature of the materials previously stored was higher than that for paper the settings of the detectors had to be changed.

- Metal sprinkler system pipes had to be replaced in one repository by plastic fittings to overcome corrosion. It was also found that the metal pipes had not been sufficiently checked on installation to ensure that they were free from dust and dirt which could block the sprinkler heads.[17]

Chapter 7

ENVIRONMENTAL CONTROL[1]

(BS 5454:2000 s.7)

Rapid changes in temperature and relative humidity, and prolonged exposure to excessive heat, light, moisture or dryness, can all cause direct damage to archival materials, and must therefore be avoided.[2] If archives are left for too long in adverse environmental conditions, the damage can become irreversible. There is a secondary risk, of infestation, where the temperature and/or relative humidity are too high, because insects and moulds which can attack archival materials thrive only in conditions of high relative humidity; they also prefer warmth.[3]

In an archive repository the aim is therefore to maintain a storage environment which is as stable as possible on a day-to-day basis, and which always remains within the specific range(s) of temperature and relative humidity recommended by BS 5454 for the respective material(s) being stored. It should also be possible to adjust the conditions if necessary (and, on grounds of energy efficiency, preferably those in individual rooms) in order to maintain stability within the recommended ranges and thus to exert the 'control' over the storage environment that is alluded to in the title of this chapter.

It remains the case that environmental control is the aspect of archive buildings where most has been determined (or most left to chance) by budgetary constraints, and where adherence to BS 5454 has been at its most selective, a blind eye often being turned, for example, to the need to filter the incoming air. For those tempted to take short cuts and settle for something less than the Standard, it is worth restating that the fundamental objective of an archive building (and any mechanical equipment used within it for purposes of environmental control) is to protect the archives against the forces which will accelerate their deterioration or otherwise put them at risk.

Fig. 8 summarises current recommendations for storage of the most common archival materials. How are these conditions to be achieved?

Assessing the options: pros and cons of air-conditioning

As already emphasised, the first question ought to be how much of the solution can be delivered by the building itself – its design, its orientation, the materials of which it is made and their configuration. The answer will of course vary according to whether it is a new build or a conversion. New buildings can, and should, be designed to deliver as much environmental stability as possible, whereas with conversions it will depend on the nature of the given structure and on any adaptations or improvements to it that are practicable and affordable. Some older buildings cannot be air-conditioned without risk of damage to the fabric.

If, according to the best calculations, the building on its own cannot deliver the required degree of stability within the approved parameters throughout the year, it will first be necessary to take stock of how serious any projected deviation from the recommendations of BS 5454 is likely to be, and whether they could be lived with or whether some form of mechanical intervention is required. This is all a matter of judgement. Whilst there should be no cause of concern for the well-being of materials in a repository which consistently meets BS 5454 recommendations, the greater and longer any anticipated deviation of storage conditions in a given building from BS 5454 recommendations the greater the cause for concern.

Any instability of temperature and relative humidity (RH) is usually measured in terms of the extent of variation above and below a chosen set point which represents the preferred storage environment. The preferred set points for paper and parchment might be, say, 17°C and 55%RH. However, no harm is likely to befall those specific materials if there is a gradual upward and downward seasonal drift[4] of the set point (for example from 16 to 18°C and back, or from 55 to 50%RH and back), provided that conditions always remain within

Fig. 8 *Environmental conditions recommended*
for the storage of various media
(Source, BS 5454:2000 s.7 and Annex A)

Material/ medium	Temperature	RH
Paper, parchment in regular use	16-19°C ± 1°C within range	45-60% ± 5% within range
Paper and parchment, little used	13-16 °C ± 1°C within range	45-60% ± 5% within range
Photographs and microfilm* - black and white - cellulose nitrate - colour	± 1°C up to: max 18 °C max 11 °C max 2 °C	30-40% 30-40% 30-40%
Moving images -black and white (safety) -black and white (nitrate) -colour	± 1 °C up to: max 16 °C max 4 °C -5 °C	35% ± 2% 50% ± 2% 30% ± 2%

*Most photographic materials can be stored at
lower, and some at slightly higher, temperature
without damage provided that the relative
humidity is adjusted correspondingly. See
McCormick-Goodhart (1996) and Adelstein
(1999).

the upper and lower limits recommended in
BS 5454. Where the materials are boxed (and
therefore to an extent benefit from their own
stable microclimate within the box) it will
not be the end of the world if, for a period
of a week or two in summer, temperature in
the repository peaks marginally above the
upper limit recommended, and then gradually
readjusts. But unfortunately there are cases,
especially in naturally climatised buildings,
where the recommended maxima or minima
are exceeded by a large amount and/or for a
prolonged period.

A caveat for certain media

It must be emphasised, however, that some
archival materials, in particular colour film,
require a stricter degree of control, and in their
case cold stores (or refrigerated containers
within a general store) may be needed to
achieve optimum storage conditions.

Ceiling-mounted fan, Norfolk

Degrees of mechanical intervention[5]

Even if it appears that some degree of
mechanical intervention will be needed to
maintain the appropriate storage conditions,
it should not automatically be assumed that a
full air-conditioning system is the only answer.
There are many variables to be addressed,
and care should be taken not to over- or to
under-specify, but rather to ensure that any
mechanical intervention is fit for purpose, and
that any equipment that is installed operates
with maximum efficiency as and when its
intervention is necessary.

It is possible to install several separate pieces
of equipment to control, for example: air
intake (ventilation, filtration to eliminate or
significantly reduce pollutants), air circulation
(ventilation, air movement to ensure consistent
environmental conditions throughout the
storage area), heating, chilling, humidification
and dehumidification. (Light is separately
considered below).

The costs of maintaining and supervising
numerous separate pieces of equipment,
however, need to be carefully evaluated
before a full air-conditioning system is ruled
out. Humidifiers, for example, have to be
rigorously maintained if they are not to
breed harmful bacteria and other micro-
organisms. Dehumidifiers, if they are not (as is
recommended) wall-mounted with an external
drain, need to be continually observed to
ensure that they do not overflow: they cannot

*Portable blower, East
Kent*

usually be safely left running unattended overnight, which may be when they are most needed. Electrostatic dust-precipitators give out ozone, a powerful corrosive agent which can break down cellulose and cause fading in materials, and must not be allowed into contact with the records.[6]

For some buildings it might well be concluded that action is required on only a limited number of fronts, for example heating in winter, a degree of assisted ventilation or air movement, and perhaps dehumidification. These, and other components such as chilling or humidification, could in some cases be supplied separately as required, and in some cases by free-standing or even portable units, and by low-tech solutions such as fans. Many buildings visited for this survey had in effect free-standing units serving individual rooms. The most unusual low-tech solution encountered, to control temperature and relative humidity for more valuable archival material in just part of a larger storage area, is the poly-tunnel at the Church of England Record Centre.

Full air-conditioning

A full air-conditioning system will in principle control all of the variables, but the implications of installing such a system need careful thought. Air-conditioning is expensive to install and maintain, and energy-intensive to run. Parts, and even entire systems, need replacing from time to time, and a life expectancy of 15 years or less is not unusual for major components. This therefore needs to be taken into account at the outset, when considering Whole-Life Cost. The custody of archives, like any public activity, cannot be undertaken without stewardship of all the costs, including the environmental costs. Against this it might be said that in some cases those costs will constitute the 'bottom line', the price that has to be paid to preserve our heritage in good order, and without which we ought not to be entering into the activity in the first place. Where an air-conditioning system is specified, it must be rigorously tested before being signed off.

Problems experienced in practice

In principle a full air-conditioning system ought to be capable of delivering a stable environment in line with BS 5454 recommendations. This has been achieved in some of the buildings visited for this study, but results in many other repositories are patchy, and problems have been reported in the great majority of buildings with full air-conditioning systems. In the case of archives, the systems need to be controllable over a wide range of 'loads', especially in relation to heating or chilling any fresh air taken in. This is a demand not usually encountered by the suppliers of eg office air-conditioning equipment, so it needs to be made clear at the outset that the requirements are very specific. For the same reason a special, not a standard, maintenance contract will also be required.

Real problems reported during this study include the following:

- Equipment wrongly specified for the volume or configuration of space to be covered, resulting either in an unstable environment or in the need for additional equipment which will take up valuable space.

- The 'engineer-knows-best' syndrome, in which, for example an engineer has

Air stacks, Devon

decided, without consulting the archivist, that only the temperature need be controlled (perhaps because stability in this respect is relatively easy to achieve), with the result that RH is all over the place on the graph.

- The contractor or sub-contractor being changed, or going bankrupt, and the new one being unable to understand what has been done so far.

- Inaccurately-measured plans that have had to be repeatedly referred back for correction.

- Equipment wrongly installed, eg certain components not connected at all, components wrongly connected to one another; the right equipment installed but in the wrong place.

- Equipment not regularly, or not correctly, maintained.

- Equipment fitted into such a cramped space that it cannot easily be accessed for monitoring or maintenance.

- Equipment installed high up in a building in such a way that it cannot be got out easily (or at all, or only at great expense involving cranes) for replacement.

- End-of-range equipment fitted because this was cheapest, but which cannot now be replaced on a like-for-like basis.

- Equipment purchased abroad on which the delivery time for new components when needed is prolonged.

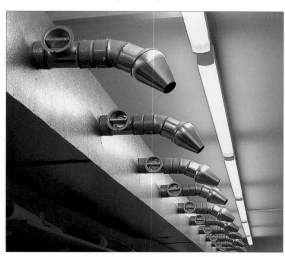

Air blowers, Warwickshire

- Under-estimation of the amount of heat generated by refrigeration equipment. This has implications in connection with the use of free-standing chilling equipment in, for example, stores for film and photographs. They are best sited near the perimeter of the building and/or provided with heat extraction facilities.

- The placement of monitoring equipment in or near air supply ducts (and nowhere else), which can result in recording the state of returned air as opposed to that circulating in the room.

Recommendations

Some practical recommendations arise from these problems and from other recent professional experiences:

- Consultants and contractors need to understand clearly what it is they are being asked to achieve and why.

- They should document what they do so that others can follow it afterwards, in case there are changes of personnel on either side during or after the contract.[7]

- Their work also needs to be effectively monitored by a competent third party before it is signed off, to ensure that they deliver a system that performs according to contract.

- It is important for the repository to maintain a log of any changes made to equipment and any servicing undertaken, with details of contractor, supplier and date.

- The specification for air-conditioning must take account of the effect of filling the storage space with archival materials. This will reduce the volume of air to be controlled (compared with the room when empty), will affect air circulation within the storage space, and could have a significant impact on the ambient relative humidity because, as noted above, many of the materials are hygroscopic.

- An air-conditioning system should not be expected to solve problems of continuing dampness in the fabric.

- In a converted building such that the walls or roof contribute little to thermal inertia, an air-conditioning system will be competing against the external conditions, is likely to be expensive to run, and may still not deliver a stable environment.

- Where space and resources permit, there is a clear advantage in having back-up machinery (stand-by or duplicate plant: BS 5454 s.7.5.1).

- Regular monitoring of the system is essential, and a continuously-running and addressable Building Management System (BMS) is very desirable. However, for this to be an effective asset there must be a strategy in place for swift response (human or mechanical) to any alarms.

- If they are not themselves in charge of the monitoring equipment and its outputs, the archivist, preservation manager or other senior member of professional staff should at least have regular access to the monitoring data.

- Lines of responsibility not only for monitoring but for any consequential action need to be clearly laid down, with an appropriate time-frame for the action.

A repository designed to rely on air-conditioning may well remain dependent on it for 24 hours a day, seven days a week throughout the year. It is unsafe to assume without careful monitoring that the equipment can with impunity be switched off at the end of the working day or at weekends and public holidays. This can present problems for repositories that are to be housed in part of a larger, shared building where the system is shut down at night.

With continuous operation, air-conditioning equipment is put under stress. It may cope with normal external conditions but prove incapable of handling prolonged extremes of weather. Where air-conditioning has been installed as an additional measure in a building which itself offers high thermal inertia, there may be a case for conducting a controlled experiment to determine what happens to the internal environment if the system is turned off from time to time. If little or no change in temperature and relative humidity results, economies may be possible by reducing the amount of regular intervention.

London Metropolitan Archives (*see case study*) has collaborated with City University

to install an energy ('power factor correction') monitor to ensure that electrical equipment is being efficiently used.

Outdoor climate[8]

The prevalent outdoor conditions of temperature, relative humidity and air quality, are currently less extreme in the UK than in many other countries, but they are not satisfactory for the storage of archives. So any building that does little to buffer its contents from the influence of the external environment is fundamentally unsuited to archive storage.

In designing archive buildings it should be remembered that there are appreciable seasonal and regional variations in Britain's climate. Some westerly areas in particular experience outdoor RH well in excess of that recommended for archive storage. Summer days everywhere can be humid, and even on rather dry days RH can climb sharply overnight. Cold winter days, by contrast, may produce low RH.[9]

Future-proofing?

A recent study by the Centre for Sustainable Heritage[10] has pointed out that if the trend of climate change is towards lower relative humidity in the summer, changes will need to be made in the design of those archive buildings intending to make the most of natural climatisation, and/or in the specifications necessary for mechanical intervention, particularly humidification. Given that new archive buildings are expected to have a *minimum* life of 20 years, the belt-and-braces approach adopted by many repositories (ie having the facility to intervene mechanically when necessary, even if it is not used all the time) has much to commend it.

Air quality and pollution

Air quality is similarly variable, but there is still localised (and sometimes more general) atmospheric pollution: for example from industrial activity and traffic exhaust gases, especially ozone and the oxides of nitrogen.[11] Pollution levels depend in part on the weather. Wind may cause pollution to travel far from its point of origin. Absence of wind, combined with strong sunlight, may cause fumes to break down into harmful pollutants. Rain, by contrast, may quickly absorb and disperse pollutant gases such as sulphur dioxide. Some pollutants may be less self-evident, like salt carried in acid droplets by winds from the sea.[12]

The Centre for Sustainable Heritage and a number of bodies overseas have conducted important new research in this period into the incidence and means of control of pollutants in the indoor museum environment, much of which is applicable to archives.[13]

Some localities may be fortunate enough to escape the worst exposure to pollutants. In some conurbations, or near busy roads or industrial activity, greater vigilance may be called for, but nowhere can be regarded as immune from periodic hazards of this kind. In some countries it is compulsory for ambient pollution levels to be tested before an archive building is erected.[14] In the United Kingdom there is no such regulation, and (in contrast with a number of other countries) with the exception of a few national repositories little research has yet been undertaken on the quality of the indoor air in our archive stores. This is another field in which solid evidence, gathered systematically over an extended period, would be welcome.

Attention needs to be paid to the siting of the air intake, and the times or external conditions in which it operates, to ensure that none of these is itself detrimental to the internal environment. This is particularly true in the case of naturally acclimatised buildings. Filtering the air through activated carbon or alumina filters (BS 5454 s.7.5.3) and washing it in plain or alkaline water[15] should reduce to insignificant levels most of the pollutants, including particulates and harmful gases.[16] Repositories which rely not on air-conditioning but on opened windows or unfiltered air vents for the supply of air, may be storing up problems, both from visible accumulations of dust and dirt and from invisible pollutant gases, whose effects may be noticeable only over a long period. Some comfort may, however, be drawn from evidence that storing archives in acid-free boxes buffers them against most of these pollutants[17] and that the fabric of the buildings can also act as an absorbent, reducing the direct threat.

Mould

Since those moulds which might choose to live off archival materials cannot survive where the relative humidity is continuously below 60%[18] it follows that where fresh

mould growth is detected in a repository RH has been exceeding that level. This is most likely to be (a) because the air handling or air-conditioning system itself is incorrectly regulated; (b) because the walls, roof or floor of the building are drawing in moisture from an outside source; or (c) because the treated air is not penetrating evenly to all parts of the storage. The problem is sometimes very localised, near external walls or directly below air-conditioning trunking. An even distribution of air may be specially difficult to achieve in large, irregularly-shaped or relatively open-plan storage areas, particularly where mobile racking is employed which, unless regularly opened and closed, may prevent the circulating air from penetrating. Mesh-ended racking may assist in this context.

Air handling: movement and air changes

There has been continued discussion during this period of the benefits of introducing some fresh air into the repository. Practice, too, has varied. At one extreme is a non-air-conditioned building where no ventilation is provided other than that caused by the opening and closing of doors and by any air leakage in the fabric (Shropshire). Some repositories (eg the Rothschild Archive) rely on the mechanical recirculation of the existing air without admitting fresh air. More commonly, a proportion of fresh air is admitted from time to time, and at the other end of this scale are a number of air-conditioned repositories where the specification is for multiple air changes per hour with a large measure of recycling but also a proportion of fresh air intake at each change. Most of these approaches can in fact result in stable temperature and relative humidity, so it becomes a question of what else needs to be considered.

Air *movement/circulation* is important in ensuring that environmental conditions remain as nearly as possible equal throughout the storage area. This should eliminate any pockets of stagnant, possibly too humid, air in the corners and along the outside walls which might otherwise encourage mould growth. The movement of the air might itself be beneficial in deterring mould growth. Movement can of course be achieved without deliberately admitting any fresh air, and it can be achieved by relatively low-tech means such as fans. The recommendation of the earlier editions of

BS 5454 that there should be six changes of air per hour was dropped in the 2000 edition, on the ground that it was not based on any proven need and could only be achieved by mechanical intervention whereas the Standard had no wish to rule out natural climatisation methods.

There is, however, another side to this, namely *air quality*. The movement of air which is in effect trapped within a sealed storage space will be less beneficial to the archives if the quality of that air falls short of what is required, for example because it is not at a suitable temperature or RH, has picked up pollutant gases from the gradual bio-deterioration of the stored materials or from other sources such as floor coverings (off-gassing), or if dust is also being picked up and circulated. However, the introduction of a certain amount of fresh air, preferably in a controlled way through filters and (in naturally climatised buildings) when external conditions permit or (in air-conditioned buildings) after appropriate conditioning, should assist in carrying away pollutants, and might make for a fresher environment for staff fetching and carrying the archives. Rates of air change as low as 1 or 2 changes per day, may well be delivered anyway by air leakage alone, and this may be sufficient to remove off-gassing. The nose can be a good monitoring instrument!

Whether natural climatisation or air-conditioning in some form is used, the repository's fabric should be as air-tight as possible so that any air coming in does so in a controlled way (at appropriate times, rates and volumes) and not simply because the fabric, or its fittings such as door and window frames, leak.[19]

Maintenance

In order to prevent direct damage to the archives and to remove a source of food for insects and other pests, regular cleaning of the repository and equipment is advisable if dust and dirt are found to be accumulating. But whenever possible dry processes (vacuuming or gentle dusting or brushing) should be used, and any damp processes reduced to the absolute minimum and at very infrequent intervals. In some new repositories with competent air filtration, it has been found that hardly any dust accumulates, and the need for cleaning is minimal.

Proper cleaning and maintenance of all heating and air-conditioning equipment, whether full, partial or free-standing, is essential to its efficient operation. It is also important for the good of the archives, the staff, visiting contractors and the public. In the most extreme case there could be a threat to life. Plant rooms in a confined space, especially if they have no air vents, may need to be monitored for harmful emissions and fitted with suitable detectors, for example for carbon monoxide.

Less obviously, a number of illnesses can be caused by organisms thriving in the equipment. Whilst the specific problems in this respect that were reported in the previous volume are not known either to have recurred or to have sprung up elsewhere, vigilance is still needed. Legionnaire's disease, potentially fatal, caused by the bacterium *legionella pneumophila*, has a penchant for heating and cooling systems but can escape in droplets into the atmosphere whence it invades the lungs. It has never been reported in an archive building in the UK, but they are not exempt from concern on that account. Other micro-organisms including bacteria and fungi can thrive in water which has not been sterilised, and some people may be susceptible to 'humidifier fever' and related ailments, so it is important periodically to drain, clean and if necessary disinfect equipment to remove all risk of infection. In hard-water areas humidifiers may also need very frequent servicing or replacement to combat scaling and ensure that they continue to function correctly.

'Sick-building syndrome' is a catch-all term, spurned by some specialists, devised to explain recurring illness among staff or public in a particular building when the cause appears to have something to do with the internal environment. Often it cannot be precisely pinned down. It seems that it may stem from either physical or psychological factors or perhaps a combination of the two. From the human point of view the availability of enough oxygen in the air supply is crucial, whether it comes by opening windows and air vents, or mechanically through an air intake system. This particularly needs to be borne in mind when it comes to public areas in the building and to staff offices. Double-glazing, insulating doors and windows to prevent draughts, and (in a converted building) blocking up old fireplaces in the interests of energy conservation can all stoke up problems if thought has not been given to alternative sources of fresh air. Human occupancy leads naturally to a build-up of carbon dioxide which if not compensated for can cause stuffiness. Air-conditioned buildings without openable windows appear more prone to complaints. Dusts, particulates and pollens may be carried through air-conditioning ducts and vents if the air intake is not properly filtered and the ducting itself not kept clean. Smoke, and smells ranging from body odours to paints, chemicals and the gases given off by furnishings, furniture and insulation materials, can contribute to the problem. Excesses of heat, cold, dryness or draught are other common complaints, and the change from one environment to another (as in the case of staff entering and leaving, or working in, cold storage areas) can be problematic to the extent that even the kind of clothing worn on such occasions needs to be taken into account. Even unaccustomed silence, for example in a storage area with no air-conditioning and nobody else present, can lead to a sense of claustrophobia or unease.

It has been shown that the human perception of 'freshness' is rather subjective and closely related to the temperature at which the individual feels most comfortable.[20] Cool, recycled air may be acceptable on a hot, stuffy day, but for much of the time people may prefer a gentle breeze through an open window, which incidentally puts them in touch with the external environment, an important psychological factor. But what quality of air are they breathing?

Ergonomic factors too affect one's view of, or allergy to, the workplace. The correct positioning of desks and tables in relation to walls, windows and workmates, the level and angle of artificial lighting or exposure to the glare of the sun, and the extent to which these can be controlled by blinds, the depth or narrowness of the field of vision and the nature of the view from the workplace – perhaps above all the extent to which one can control one's own working environment – all contribute to the overall well-being of the building's occupants, and to what might be called the 'well building syndrome'. It is the task first of planners and then of management to ensure that this is achieved and maintained.

Ideally the environmental conditions recommended in BS 5454 should be maintained everywhere in the building where records are being consulted or worked on, but (as with lighting) some compromise is inevitable for human comfort. A few conservation workshops are now provided with air-conditioning regulated for the good of the records. In public areas, openable windows are a useful aid to ventilation, and have been provided even in some air-conditioned buildings. To improve ventilation quickly or for short periods without leaving windows open, fans may be useful.

Light[21]

BS 5454:2000 (s.8 and 13.2) places more emphasis than the previous editions on the protection of archives against excessive exposure to light, both when in regular use in staff office and reading rooms, and more especially when on exhibition. Exposure to light, especially but not exclusively ultra-violet light, contributes to the ageing of most archival materials. Damage is directly proportional to the intensity and duration of the exposure, and is irreversible.

The contribution of the building itself to the control of sunlight has already been discussed. A number of record offices including those in Berkshire and Norfolk have automatic electronic blinds on the search room and staff office windows, in the first case fitted externally and in the second internally, to restrict strong sunlight. Many others have manually operated blinds as necessary, and windows are often either made of glass which incorporates ultra-violet filtration or covered internally with an anti u/v film.

Electric lighting, no less than natural light, has environmental implications within an archive building, and of course contributes to the expenditure of energy. A good deal of practical guidance is available, both in BS 5454 and in the text books, on such matters as lighting levels for storage and exhibition and for the consultation of records in the search room. In storage areas, archives in boxes are not going to come to any harm if the lights are left on for long periods, but lighting may contribute to heat gain and the practice of leaving lights on throughout the working day for the convenience of staff is costly in energy terms and should be critically examined. It is helpful if all lights which have to be switched off out of hours can be controlled from a central point.

Lighting triggered in different zones by movement sensors when anyone enters the zone has been widely introduced. However, this can be inconvenient if it switches off automatically (because it has detected no movement) when there is actually someone still working in the room. For this reason some still prefer a manually-operated pull-cord system for the lights. Sensor-operated lighting is not recommended for use in staff offices or conservation workshops where delicate operations or other important work may have to be interrupted while the lights are re-activated. At the Royal Academy, where archives are stored in cabinets, lighting is triggered when the cabinet doors are opened.

In search rooms, the use of up-lighting can avoid bright light falling on the documents and provide a good ambient light. Areas set aside for the consultation of microforms are generally provided with more subdued lighting so that the screens can be easily read, and for maximum flexibility dimmer switches can be fitted to the main lighting controls.

Chapter 8

CONVERSION OF EXISTING BUILDINGS[1]

The pros and cons

Ideally, decisions on future archive accommodation would be made dispassionately and without constraints, so that all options could be carefully evaluated. But in practice the decision whether to opt for a purpose-build or conversion of an existing building that was conceived for some other purpose are of course often heavily influenced by political and financial constraints: by the relative priority and prestige accorded to the archive service in the eyes of its governing authority, by tightly restricted budgets and by other competing claims upon capital resources and land.

Planning a purpose-built repository ought in principle to give archivist and architect more scope to make specifications in line with BS 5454 for every aspect of the development. Site and orientation can be used to best advantage. There will be more control over design, structure, materials, layout, the internal environment, and the furnishings, equipment and lines of communication that make for a pleasant and efficient working environment. The architect should be able to design the space to fit the operation, rather than the other way round.[2]

The archivist whose only practical option is to look for a building to convert should bear in mind first that 'conversion' is the operative word: some degree of real adaptation will be necessary because buildings do not come ready-made for archive storage; and secondly that even in a conversion the aim should be to match as nearly as possible what could be achieved in a purpose-built building. It boils down to this: will any compromises that have to be made in order to convert that particular building to archival use – such as any deviations from the recommendations of BS 5454 – be prejudicial to the records and/or the users?

For all that, there can be advantages in the conversion of an existing building. For example:

- It could be significantly cheaper than a purpose-build.

- It could be the only way to obtain a town-centre site, a site immediately adjacent to other offices of the parent authority, or for that matter any site at all.

- It could be quicker than commissioning new work. (This might, for example, suit the needs of a service seeking temporary or relatively short-term accommodation pending a move to more permanent premises.)

- Broadly speaking, in the case of a conversion the building's advantages and disadvantages will be apparent in advance, whereas in the case of new buildings they may be difficult to visualise from the drawing board, or may only become apparent after occupancy.

- It could provide an opportunity to rescue a redundant building that is architecturally interesting, thereby minimising the call upon new land or material resources.[3] A dignified historic building might in turn benefit the archive service's image. However, buildings of historic interest do not *ipso facto* make ideal repositories for historic records, nor should the romantic notion be fostered that archives are somehow happier if stored in old buildings. Each case has to be judged on its own merits. Age is certainly not of itself a disadvantage (*see case studies for Denbighshire, Oxfordshire, St George's Chapel Windsor*), but not all old buildings are of a suitable calibre.

The main issues

Important issues to be addressed before opting for a conversion include:

Site

The site should be evaluated as in Chapter 3 above, but as the building is already in place special attention must be paid to any drawbacks of the location itself, including any limitations on the ease of access for readers, for staff and for the delivery of documents. Is there space for subsequent expansion if required?

Neighbours

Are the premises free-standing, or built on to one or more properties, or just part of a larger building? Who are the neighbours/co-tenants? Are any of their activities actually or potentially incompatible with the purposes of an archive building?

Size, shape and general 'fit'

How big is the building, what shape and how many storeys? Is the area/volume sufficient for the projected needs of the archive service? If it is too big, what will be done with the unwanted space and what risks attend that use? Can the building be heated/cooled economically and efficiently? If it is too small, are there possibilities for lateral or vertical extension, now or in future? Is there going to be space enough to fit in all the functions envisaged for the building, or will it be the proverbial quart in a pint pot? Are there sensible lines of communication horizontally and vertically, or are new measures going to be needed, such as the installation of lifts? Is there enough circulating space (corridors etc) to obviate going through one function to reach another?

Robustness

What was the building's former use? Did that require similar floor loadings, fire-proofing and levels of security to those that will be needed for the archive service? If not can it be easily adapted to meet the new requirements? If it was not designed with heavy loads in mind, will the foundations and floor loadings be sufficient? Has the building been well maintained, or are there any signs of defects such as leaking roofs, damp walls (resulting, for example, from gutters blocked by falling leaves), crumbling or flaking masonry, eroded stone or brickwork? Can the defects be made good within an acceptable time-frame? Are there likely to be recurrent high costs for maintenance, given the age or nature of the building?

Adaptability

How freely may the building be altered? For example, is it subject to Listed Building or other planning constraints? Could it be air-conditioned without risk to the fabric? If the building is not to be owned by the parent authority but only leased, will the landlord allow any necessary alterations? How important is it to preserve the building's original character, or conversely to work for major change? How is the available space currently sub-divided? Will this compartmentation suit the new requirements or can it be altered? Will it be possible to house the archive service's various functions conveniently and efficiently? Are the floors of adjacent rooms at an identical level or are there awkward steps or ramps?

Services

Can the needs of the archive service be met in respect of services and utilities (water, drainage and sewerage, power supplies, telephone, wireless reception etc), either from those already in situ or through new work? Conversely, are there existing installations which will need overhauling, replacing or removing (eg heating systems, fire suppression and alarm systems, water pipes in the wrong places)?

Image

What image of the archive service will that building convey to the local community and to the archive service users?

Spotting potential hazards[4]

Is there anything else about the structure of the building that might prove difficult or inconvenient if not managed to the advantage of the service? Consider, for example:

- *basic structure and materials*: excessive amounts of wood (fire hazard); flimsy warehouse-type cladding (risk of damage to fabric from exterior); poor insulation (loss of heat); asbestos used in walls, ceilings and lagging (health and safety); poor air-tightness generally (difficult to maintain stable environment; risk of dust, pests and pollutants)

- *roofs*: flimsy or fragile (environmental and security hazards); multiple gables, valley gutters (prone to blockage, damp); poor insulation

- *windows*: too many and/or too large (light, security); skylights (leaks, intruders, heat gain/loss)

- *internal walls*: flaking or crumbling (dust)
- *fireplaces and chimneys* (fire, environmental hazard)
- *ceilings*: very high (waste of space, heat); very low (restricted racking, air circulation, services)
- *columns or other structural supports* (restricted freedom of manoeuvre)
- *compartmentation*: many small rooms (will this suit handling, management requirements?)

- *basement accommodation*: inadequate drainage (flooding, damp).

There is no short cut to subjecting a building to a thorough test along these lines. Some will emerge triumphant. Others may seem just right as buildings but be in an impossible location; or they may be ideally located but hopeless for the task. Many will be suitable in most respects but have a few unavoidable inconveniences, and the question will then arise whether the inconveniences can be mitigated, compensated for by other provisions, or reluctantly accepted,

Greenwich Heritage Centre: part of former royal arsenal.

Carmarthenshire: former school

or whether the building must be rejected. The last might be a painful decision, because it will mean going back to square one, but it must not be ruled out.

Building types converted 1993-2005

Fig. 9, although not absolutely comprehensive, notes many of the types of building that have been converted to archival use in this period. The list could have been greatly extended had it taken account of *in situ* conversions: that is, the adaptation or refurbishment of another part of the building in which the archives were already housed, which has been a common development in university and public libraries, and in certain museums.

A note on warehouses and industrial buildings

As in the period covered by the previous volume, warehouses and other former industrial premises have again proved to be the types of building most commonly converted for archival use. Almost all the business archives considered for his survey are housed in such premises (BT, Barclays, Guardian/Observer, News International, Unilever), but a number of other examples are mentioned below. Warehouses come in many shapes and forms depending on the nature of the goods formerly stored: single and multi-storey; built to last for ever, or purely to provide functional shelter as cheaply as possible; designed for commodities with high, or with low, value; offering strict, or only limited, security. Their former use may give important clues to the standards to which the buildings must have been designed, for example in security, floor-loading and fire-resistance, and this in turn may say something of their likely suitability as archive buildings.

Here, age may prove an advantage. Georgian or Victorian brick warehouses can be fortress-like (*see case studies: Guardian/Observer, North West Film Archive*), built to last. Their thick walls contribute to the stability of the internal environment. In contrast, many recently constructed warehouses, of the concrete block and corrugated metal variety in particular, are altogether flimsier, and more transitory in concept. These are unlikely to help maintain environmental stability for the stored archives, which might therefore only be achievable at quite a cost (if at all), because in the absence of significant mass in the structure,

Type of building	Examples
Warehouse	Ayrshire, Barclays Group, Devon, Gloucestershire, Guardian/Observer News International
Other industrial building (etc)	BT (telephone exchange), Deepstore (salt mine); Unilever (factory building)
Church (or part of church)	East Riding, Oxfordshire, Birmingham RC archdiocese, Brentwood RC diocese
School	Carmarthenshire, Gwynedd (Dolgellau), Leicestershire
House/ domestic premises	Diageo, Dumfries, Elgar Birthplace, Reading University Museum of English Rural Life (hall of residence)
Shop/ department store	Wolverhampton, Worcestershire Family History Centre
Police station	Cumbria (Whitehaven)
Gaol	Denbighshire
Other historic buildings	Gonville & Caius College Cambridge Greenwich (part of Royal Arsenal) Royal Archives Windsor (within Castle) St George's Chapel Windsor (undercroft) Wirral (town hall)

Fig. 9   Conversions
Examples of types of buildings converted to archival use 1993-2005
(Note: for the most part this list excludes refurbishment of existing accommodation, in situ conversions of library and museum premises, and the colonisation of additional parts of a building already used for archive storage)

and often the lack of insulation, the internal environment responds very closely to that outside. Heat will tend to escape in winter, and be gained in summer.

Hybrid solutions combining conversion and purpose-building

The choice is not always and automatically limited to purpose-building *or* conversion, as the following examples will show.

- The Record Office for Leicestershire, Leicester and Rutland (*see case study*) acquired a former school which it converted

Royal Society of Arts: new reading room alongside converted building

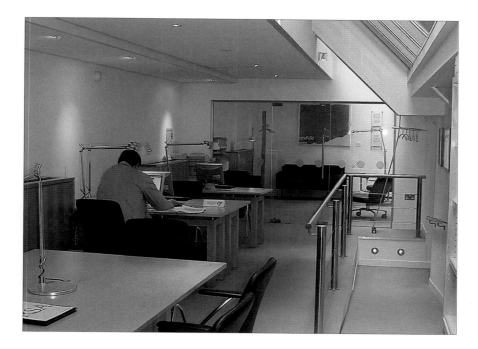

to provide accommodation for public services, conservation workshop and staff offices; a new purpose-built storage block was constructed in the grounds.

- English Heritage's National Monuments Record repository (*see case study*) is purpose-built, linked to converted GWR railway offices which house the staff and public services.

- Diageo plc converted a former distiller's house into public search room, display rooms and staff offices, and built on to it first one and then a second warehouse for archive storage.

- Gloucestershire Record Office (*see case study*), having run out of space within its own grounds for further expansion, acquired an immediately adjacent warehouse that had stood empty for a number of years. It retained the walls and roof of the warehouse as an outer shell and, in modular fashion as resources allowed, built a number of archive storage units, or 'pods', within the space. Similar developments, but on a smaller scale and with varying degrees of mechanical intervention, may be seen, for example, at Barclays Group Archives and News International.

- The Devon Record Office and National Meteorological Archive (*see case study*)

occupies rather more than half of a very large warehouse, the remainder having been developed simultaneously to house other county council functions. As in Gloucestershire, the archive storage is in effect purpose built, free-standing within the shell, and not touching either walls or roof of the outer building.

- University College London Special Collections Department is, at the time of writing, temporarily occupying a converted warehouse. Inside this is a small free-standing room for items requiring a greater degree of environmental control or security.

Birmingham RC archdiocese: converted crypt

Diageo exterior: new storage block added on to converted house

Specific problems reported from buildings converted 1993-2005

The checklists given above for evaluating buildings are largely based on the direct experience of archivists in converted buildings occupied since 1977. The following additional points to be aware of are among the specific problems reported from buildings visited in the course of the present survey. *It should be noted that some of these problems could equally befall purpose-built accommodation if not taken into account at the planning stage.*

Structure

- heavy maintenance costs (in a historic building)

- poor insulation or poor airtightness

- damp from leaks repaired before occupancy has continued to emerge afterwards and disfigure the walls

- pillars have had to be planned around

- structural metal racking uprights (in a library) could not be removed or re-sited

- condensation, eg drips from the roof, or interstitial condensation (ie within the building fabric itself)

- image: it does not look like an archive building, and people pass it by.

Site and orientation

- too much sun in reading room or conservation workshop

- isolated site: some worries for staff and readers late at night; maintenance etc often postponed by parent body

- adjacent woodland or garden: gutters blocked by leaf-fall; external air intake blocked by foliage

- flood risk

- no perimeter fence: repository wall damaged by a reversing lorry.

Environmental control

- impossible to maintain stability within BS 5454 even with air-conditioning because building fabric is flimsy and 'leaks'.

Size, shape and layout

- awkward configuration, eg long trek from loading bay to document reception; criss-crossing of search room to reach staff offices; receptionist isolated from rest of staff

- some essential functions omitted because the building was not large enough (interview room, sufficient staff offices, general storage space)

Barclays group

- restricted site: no space for future expansion

- forced to locate public functions upstairs, not from choice but because insufficient space adjacent to main entrance on ground floor.

A note on shared premises

In some of the cases studied for this survey (and others not mentioned) the archive service occupies only part of a larger building. This is the norm in the case of local authority and university libraries and national and local museums, irrespective of whether the building is purpose-built or a conversion.

Sharing can be beneficial to both staff and public when it unites under one roof kindred reference and cultural services. Sharing may also be beneficial to under-resourced services if there can be some exchange between, for example, library and archives staff to cover at peak hours or during staff leave.

The security, storage and environmental requirements specific to the archives must however be separately planned and monitored. Shared accommodation may prove problematic if it leaves outside the archivist's responsibility the control of the other parts of the building and the activities carried on there, some of which might represent potential hazards to the archives. This is particularly true if those activities are carried on outside the opening hours of the repository.

If space in the overall development is very tight, there can also be a danger of the archive service (which as already stated needs ample space for expansion) being boxed in.

CONCLUSION

Although many cautionary tales have been told in these pages, the overall purpose of this volume is certainly not to deter, but rather to encourage all those engaged in the planning and implementation of archive building projects. It should also help equip them to face up to critical building-related issues such as fitness for purpose, sustainability, and the responsible use of energy and resources without necessarily always aspiring to the most (apparently) 'high-tech' solutions.

There is every reason to celebrate the progress made in the UK in this period. And we can look forward to the opening of other new archive buildings that were nearing completion as this book went to press, among them those for Coventry, the East Riding of Yorkshire, the John Rylands University Library of Manchester, Northumberland and Shetland. Still more were at earlier stages of planning and development. It is hoped that they and others who follow in their footsteps (if the funding can be found in an increasingly competitive environment) will be able to draw on guidance given here and to learn from the practical experience of those who have gone before them.

Looking to the future, it is clear that, as far as storage is concerned, greater provision will be needed for archives that are 'born digital', and that archive services to the public will have to take more account of online access and wireless technology. On the basis of the buildings studied for this project, it still seems optimistic to suppose that a large repository in the UK can achieve conformity with the recommendations of BS 5454 as to temperature and relative humidity without some form of mechanical intervention (often including cooling, since in almost every case it is high summer temperatures that cause the greatest problems). Nevertheless, all archive buildings should be designed to achieve high thermal inertia, not only to assist in maintaining stable storage conditions for the archives but also to keep running costs and energy consumption in check. More research on the indoor air quality of our archive buildings, both naturally and mechanically acclimatised, would be useful.

The Case Studies that follow in Part Two pick up many of the themes addressed in Part One. They have been selected to give a reasonable geographical spread throughout the UK and to represent each of the main sectors: national, local authority, university, business and specialist repositories. A short section of simplified plans for selected repositories follows the case studies.

PART TWO

CASE STUDIES in alphabetical order

British Library (London)
Cambridge University, Churchill Archive Centre extension
Cambridge University, Girton College, Duke Building
Cardinal Tomás Ó Fiaich Memorial Library and Archive (Armagh)
Cumbria Record Office and Local Studies Library, Whitehaven
Denbighshire Record Office (Ruthin)
Devon Record Office and National Meteorological Archive (Exeter)
English Heritage, National Monuments Record (Swindon)
Essex Record Office (Chelmsford)
Film Archives:
>   Northern Region Film and TV Archive (Middlesbrough)
>   North West Film Archive (Manchester)
>   Yorkshire Film Archive (York)
Glasgow University Library Special Collections
Gloucestershire Record Office extension (Gloucester)
Guardian and Observer Newsroom, archive and visitor centre (London)
Hereford Cathedral Library and Archives
Leicestershire, Leicester and Rutland, Record Office for (Leicester)
London Metropolitan Archives
National Archives of Scotland, Thomas Thomson House (Edinburgh)
National Library of Wales (Aberystwyth)
Norfolk Record Office and East Anglia Film Archive (Norwich)
Orkney Library and Archive (Kirkwall)
Oxfordshire Record Office (Oxford)
Perth and Kinross Council Archive (Perth)
St George's Chapel Archives and Chapter Library, Windsor
Shropshire Records and Research Centre (Shrewsbury)
Southampton University Library Special Collections
Surrey History Centre (Woking)
Tameside Local Studies and Archives Centre (Ashton under Lyne)
Tate Gallery Library and Archive, Hyman Kreitman Research Centre (London)
The National Archives (Kew)
Unilever Archives (Port Sunlight)
University of Warwick Modern Records Centre and BP Archives (Coventry)
Warwickshire Record Office (Warwick)
York University Borthwick Institute for Archives

Appendix:

Jersey Archive
Published references for UK archive buildings not featured as case studies
Simplified plans of selected UK archive buildings
Archive building projects in the UK completed 1993-2005 (checklist)

British Library

St Pancras, London NW1

Purpose-built, opened in stages, 1997-1999

Much has been spoken and written about the magnificent British Library building at St Pancras which first opened to the public in 1997 after more than twenty years' gestation and was officially opened by the Queen in 1998. It is so much more than an 'archive building' that it is difficult to encompass within a book of this kind. But an 'archive building' in part indeed it is and, measured in terms of linear, square, or cubic capacity, the provision made here for storage of, and access to archives and manuscripts puts it in the top league in the United Kingdom.

This case study is limited to those parts of the building that are devoted to the care and study of archives and manuscripts, which for the most part means the accommodation provided respectively for Manuscripts and for the India Office Records. These cannot be fully judged in isolation from those other functions such as conservation workshops, exhibition galleries and the conference centre which are shared across all the Library's departments but which are not discussed here.

None of the archive accommodation is immediately identifiable from the piazza in front of the building. Storage for this purpose, unlike that for printed books, is predominantly above ground, and for the most part cocooned within thick internal brick walls and behind fire doors.

The reading room for the India Office Records (part of the Pacific and Asia Collections) is approached through a single-storey reference area which opens up into a lofty and airy space several storeys high for the main reading area, its large windows being fitted with sun blinds. The room seats around 90 readers, with a considerable open-access library to one side. Portraits and a number of model ships from the East India Company complete the ambience. The Manuscripts reading room, with seats for about 60 readers, has a rather different character. Here, natural light is admitted only indirectly, through recessed skylights above some of the tables, and from the clerestory windows above the balcony which are not visible from the readers' tables. Electric up-lighting reflected from the ceiling properly respects the needs of the manuscripts for protection from over-exposure, but some readers have found it rather dim.

The storage areas for the two departments are distinct, although in places they are contiguous, separated only by metal caging, a concept that owes more to traditional library than to archival practice. The great variety of physical forms and sizes of the archives and manuscripts held, which range from ancient papyri to modern letters, and from seals and scrolls to maps, plans and heavy bound volumes, demands a commensurate assortment of purpose-designed racking. For the India Office Records this is a mixture of mobile and static racking, for Manuscripts entirely static, partly on account of the floor-loading capacity.

Fire prevention strategy is based first on the overall compartmentation of the building, in which individual zones can be isolated. Water sprinklers are fitted throughout, except in the inner safe rooms, designed for rarer or more valuable items, where an Inergen® gas system is installed. Full air-conditioning is provided, specified in accordance with BS 5454.

During the lengthy gestation period for the British Library's building, unforeseen factors led to many important changes to the initial specifications. Not the least of these was the absorption of the India Office Records within the British Library organisation and the need to find appropriate space for that. Consequently as the project developed some of the space had to be adapted to suit these new requirements, and equally the departments themselves sometimes had to adapt their own plans in order to fit the available spaces. Although this has led to a few inconveniences, most of the initial problems have been solved and this is excellent accommodation of which the nation can be proud.

Architect: Colin St John Wilson.
Published references: C StJ Wilson, *The design and construction of the British Library* (1998). R Stonehouse and G Stromberg, *The architecture of the British Library at St Pancras* (2004), which includes detailed plans of the building (pp.52ff and Appendix). C Kitching, 'Preservation in new buildings', in *LIBER Quarterly*, 10 (2000), no. 3, pp.376-86.

Cambridge University:
Churchill Archives Centre extension
Churchill College, Cambridge

Purpose-built, 2002

The first building for the Archives Centre at Churchill College was opened in 1973. Although it was designed before even the first edition of BS 5454 (1977), it might well have been featured in the previous volume of ABUK as a good example of the design of the period. It substantially met the recommendation of BS 5454, and indeed continues after more than a quarter of a century to provide robust and useful storage, together with public search room, an exhibition space, a conservation workshop and staff offices.

The extension was opened by Lady Thatcher and houses her papers. Clad in matching brick on a steel and concrete frame, and linked by a glazed bridge to the original building, it is of heavy mass and insulation. It provides storage accommodation on four floors, fully air-conditioned but treated as a single volume for purposes of air handling and fire-suppression (using an automatic Inergen® gas system). In a college where the water-tightness of flat roofs has already proved challenging, a slightly sloping roof was preferred in order to assist drainage. The gentle fall of the land towards the site, and the consequent risk of water accumulating at the foot of the building called for specific design, drainage and structural precautions, including the provision of a slatted metal floor in the basement, to facilitate inspection. No problems have yet been experienced. Interest has been added to an otherwise plain brick exterior wall by the addition of a horizontal band of Portland stone bearing a fine monumental inscription by the Cardozo Kindersley Workshop, Cambridge, recording the principal benefactors who made the building possible. A light-well on the corner of the building is fitted with a symbolic

'butterfly' of angled glass plates extending to the full height of the building and standing proud of it. Protective bollards have had to be installed beside it.

As part of the same overall development in 2001-2002 the existing conservation workshop was refurbished to the conservator's own specifications. Although its long and narrow shape requires all the equipment to be placed against the walls it is well equipped for an archive of this size. The glazed roof of the workshop causes some heat gain in summer; improvements are under consideration, but meanwhile conditions are regulated by wall-mounted air-conditioning units.

The public search room, housing the Stephen Roskill Library, was also refurbished and subdivided into two named working areas separated by glass screens, with a smaller microfilm reading room off. About a dozen readers can be accommodated in comfort.

Architects: tcc, Cambridge.
Cost: c.£2 million.
Storage: c.4.5 km.

Cambridge University:
Girton College, Duke Building

Purpose-built, 2005

This single-storey L-shaped extension to the
college library forms two sides of Campbell
Court adjacent to the college chapel, and
was designed to respond sensitively to the
original buildings by Alfred Waterhouse. The
axis of the 'L' connected to the main library
accommodates an ICT room with seats for
16 readers, and associated staff offices. This
part of the building is a lightweight steel-
framed structure and has a flat roof sown with
sedum. The ICT room is separated by a thick
double-glazed screen from the second axis of
the new building, which houses in succession
the archivist's office, the Littler reading room
for archives and special book collections, a
suite of rooms for conservation, the archives
and special collections strongroom and finally,
entered from the outside, a small plant room.

The reading room, with seats for a dozen
readers, has a polished oak floor. In the
centre, below the readers' tables, a specially-
commissioned rug designed by Kate Blee
and woven in central Turkey adds a touch

of colour and warmth. Externally-mounted terracotta fins are angled in such a way that no direct sunlight falls on the readers' tables, whilst ensuring that those seated at the tables still have a good view of the gardens. The conservation/preservation suite is unusual, comprising three separate small rooms, each with a window into the next. This arrangement is well suited to a small archive, as it allows wet and dry, and clean and dirty functions to be undertaken without one impinging on another in this confined space.

For the strongroom, the architect's initial intention had been to create a completely passively-controlled environment, and indeed it is the building's substantial mass and insulation that does most of the work of stabilising the storage environment. The strongroom comprises an inner 'box' of heavy construction, with dense masonry walls and a concrete floor and roof. This meets a very high standard of airtightness and is thermally insulated to a high level. The outer shell, from which it is separated, comprises an elegant skin of specially-made red brick, complementing the library and adjacent college buildings. The gently pitched roof is covered with four stepped layers of lead.

After discussion with engineers the design was slightly modified to allow for more mechanical intervention when external conditions exceeded the limits of the 'heavyweight' construction to maintain the stability specified by BS 5454:2000. Air is taken into the storage area from concealed vents in the courtyard outside. It is ducted below ground, which helps to keep the air cool, and when necessary it is further chilled on entry to the building. This approach reduces the energy required for both cooling (by 54%) and heating (by 23%) of the input air. When visited, six months after its official opening, stable conditions within BS 5454 recommendations had been achieved by this semi-passive method of control, which might well commend itself to other small repositories. Fire protection is by means of an Argonite® gas system.

Architects: Allies and Morrison, whose assistance in the preparation of this case study is gratefully acknowledged.
Cost: around £2.5 million, including a donation of £500,000 by Miss Alison Duke.
Photo of windows courtesy of Allies & Morrison

Cardinal Tomás Ó Fiaich Memorial Library and Archive
Armagh

Purpose-built, 1999

This building, which houses the Roman Catholic diocesan archives for Armagh and a number of other archives as well as the cardinal's own specialist collections, is prominently situated atop Ara Coeli, the hillside site of the RC cathedral. Beyond the grass which slopes away from the building, the Library's perimeter is distinctively demarcated by ornamental iron railings, whilst from the front gate the cathedral's spires can just be seen beyond the Library's roofline. The hipped lead roof, which has generously overhanging eaves to protect much of the building from direct sunlight, nicely complements the blue-grey limestone of the walls. Although the building is laid out on a basically rectangular floor plan, many of its internal features are full of visual interest and far from four-square.

Functions are segregated in three parallel rows from the front to the back of the building. An external porch with heavy bronze-clad doors leads to an engraved glass internal door into a lofty and bright reading room which rises to the full height of the building. Beams, columns and angled supports for the sloping roof are left exposed to view. At the apex, a long row of roof-light windows runs the full width of the building and provides much of the natural light for the reading room and staff offices below. Electric lighting is from suspended up-lights. At one end of the reading area, sliding partitions separate off a lecture/exhibition/meeting room, but the whole of this front section can be opened up into one if required. Behind the reception desk in the centre of the room a low screen wall,

substantially glazed, demarcates the second tier of functions: the offices and workrooms for librarian and archivist, and the public WCs. Beyond this again, two strongrooms occupy the full width of the rear portion of the building, one intended for books and one for archives. These rooms are inter-connected, but may be entered respectively from the librarian's and the archivist's workroom through secure fire doors. Both rooms are air-conditioned by means of wall-mounted units. They have shallow clerestory windows below the eaves of the building, well above the height of the mobile racking. The whole building, including the strongrooms, is fitted with water sprinklers, smoke detectors and intruder alarms.

A grant from the Heritage Lottery Fund covered something like two-thirds of the building's total cost of around £900,000 and ensured that it could be fitted out and finished to a high standard. This decision has been well rewarded in a building that combines essential simplicity with fit-for-purpose functionality and will be the envy of many small specialist repositories.

Architects: P & B Gregory, Belfast.
Published references: 'The Cardinal Tomás Ó Fiaich Memorial Library and Archive', in *Seanchas Ard Mhaca*, 17 no 2 (1998), pp.167-8. CEB Brett, *Buildings of County Armagh*, (Belfast, Ulster Architectural Heritage Society, 1999), pp.230-1.

Cumbria Record Office and Local Studies Library
Scotch Street, Whitehaven

Converted former police station, 1996

A former police station ought to be a safe bet as a sturdy and secure building for archives. So, in general, this has proved to be.

The original mid-Victorian shell of red sandstone was retained, with minimal intervention other than the blocking up of some of the windows. The building was re-roofed in slate, and an adjacent magistrate's court was demolished, making room for a small car park, entered through the archway to the former fire station which once stood next door. The inside of the old police station was gutted and re-designed, on two floors, with archive reception and storage on the ground floor and public services and staff offices on the first floor. A new entrance porch was added between the two wings at the front of the building, equipped with a video entry phone to enable staff to control admittance from the first floor. This is perhaps a bit off-putting for some first-time visitors, but it avoids the need to employ a separate receptionist.

The search room, on the first floor, which serves both archives and local studies, is impressively spacious, with seating for 24 readers at tables, and a further 22 using microforms. It is well provided with both natural and artificial light. A section in the centre opens right up to the inside of the pitched roof and has effective up-lighting. The room can be divided into two by a folding sound-proof partition to provide separate lecture or meeting facilities. The single adjacent office, shared by all the staff, although it is conveniently located, was always ungenerous in size, and no room is available for confidential interviews.

The single archive strongroom, on the ground floor, is windowless with a perimeter wall of concrete blocks inside the outer stone wall. The room is fully air-conditioned and fitted with smoke detectors and alarms and intruder alarms. An adjacent area serves for document reception and assessment and has an external door for deliveries.

Even though it took a little longer, and cost rather more than expected to make the building fully waterproof, this was (and remains) an economical and cost-effective investment by the County Council, as a branch office of the archive service. It is now in effect full, although there is space to expand on site when resources permit.

Architects: in-house.
Cost: c.£700,000.
Storage: 172 cu.m.

Denbighshire Record Office
Clwyd Street, Ruthin

Converted former gaol, 2002

Ruthin gaol, which was decommissioned in 1916, has been put to various subsequent uses. For its conversion into a munitions factory during the Second World War, the space between the galleries at each level of the main cell block was filled in with new floors carried on steel joists. Much of the character of the original building was thereby lost. Subsequently it was used by the library, and from 1972 (with relatively minor alterations to the structure), for the storage of archives. Clwyd Record Office, as it then was, established a public search room on the ground floor in 1980, using the cells on either side of this, as well as those above, for the storage of archives: an awkward arrangement in a number of respects, but the best that could be managed without major expense.

In 1998 a bid was made to the Heritage Lottery Fund to develop the site: on the one hand to provide a much needed facelift for the record office, and a new Ruthin Gaol heritage attraction, and on the other hand to restore this fine historic building to its former glory. The conversion included stripping out the flooring added by the munitions factory, providing a new roof and reinstating roof lights in their original position, fitting new iron railings around the galleries, based on the design of the originals, and clearing the courtyard of low-grade buildings to make an attractive open space.

Conversion work was delayed by the serious flooding of 2000 in the area, but was eventually completed in 2002 thanks to many funding partners (see below). The opportunity was taken significantly to alter the location of functions within the various buildings. The document reading room was moved from its cell block to the former prison chapel, which has provided a pleasant working environment for up to 16 readers. The two cell blocks (of 1820 and 1866) were completely refurbished and a new full air-conditioning system was installed throughout, with an Inergen® fire-suppression system. The original plans of the Victorian (Pentonville-style) block revealed that

there was a built-in ventilation system within its walls and floors which could be used as part of the strategy for delivering air within the new system. The central part of the ground floor now no longer has its own 'ceiling', but opens right up to the roof three storeys above. At ground level one end of the cell block forms part of the heritage trail, divided by a glass screen from the majority of that floor where the remaining cells, completely re-cabled, provide microfilm and computer access points for record office readers, as well as access to catalogues and indexes. The two floors of galleries above, which are now visible from the ground floor, are given over to archive storage, in a multiplicity of individual (or sometimes double) cells. The topmost level, below the new roof, houses the air handling plant. With the exception of one space given over to the reception of archives, cleaning and boxing, the cells in the basement are the main part of the heritage attraction, giving an insight into the history of the building and of prison life. The earlier cell block is given over to archive storage, on two floors. The environmental conditions throughout the storage areas broadly conform to BS 5454 recommendations, but the older block is taking longer than the Victorian one to settle down fully.

The administrative block at the front of the site has been developed to provide, on the ground floor, a new reception point for readers, a general staff office, and a small locker-room-cum-refreshment space for readers, whilst on the first floor there is a suite of staff offices.

This imaginative and cost-effective re-use of a worthwhile historic building has provided much improved facilities for the record office.

Architects: in-house.
Cost: about £3 million in all, including the heritage attraction. Funding partners in addition to the County Council were the Heritage Lottery Fund (£1.3 million), the Welsh Development Agency, the Wales Tourist Board, CADW and the European Regional Development Fund.
Storage: capacity about 250 cu.m of which 190 cu.m. is currently occupied.

Devon Record Office and National Meteorological Archive
Great Moor House, Exeter

Purpose-built within the shell of a converted warehouse, 2005 (See Appendix for plan)

Devon County Council purchased Great Moor House, a very large former BT warehouse on the outskirts of Exeter (51,000 sq ft plus 21,000 sq ft office accommodation), in 1998. The building, clad in fairly standard warehouse profiled steel composite, was considerably larger than the Record Office alone required. A partnership was struck with the Meteorological Office to move its archive into the building. Other county functions (including library headquarters, school library service, curriculum services, learning resources, youth music, and IT training) were eventually to occupy the remainder.

Much of the shell of the original warehouse, including the roof, was retained intact, although in places windows had to be inserted to allow natural light for offices and public services, and a new glazed entrance lobby was built, at the 'rear' in terms of the original building, next to a generous car park, and with a Park and Ride car park for the city alongside.

A 2-hour fire wall was built internally along almost the full length of the building's spine, reaching from the floor to the apex of the roof. To one side of this were located all the functions unrelated to the archive services, plus some of the public services for archives, whilst to the other side of the wall a new two-storey archive storage block was constructed, within the overall warehouse space but having its own 4-hr fire walls and concrete slab roof. This block is separated by a perimeter corridor from the outer walls of the warehouse and also from the spinal fire wall, nor does its roof meet the roofline of the warehouse. A second skin has been added below the upper roof, with insulation in between, to assist thermal stability.

Storage comprises a series of discrete strongrooms separated by fire walls. Most rise through the full two storeys, the upper floor being separated from the lower by galvanised steel gratings so that each two-storey 'room' is treated as a single space for air-handling, whereas for access there are separate fire doors on each of the two levels, constructed in wood but with additional outer steel roller doors on fusible links for use in an emergency. The repository is of heavy mass and insulation. The internal climate of the storage areas has been designed to be largely self-regulating by passive means. There is little mechanical intervention. Four ventilation stacks rise through the store rooms and up to the outer roof where they are angled to face the four winds. A BMS controls air intake, at times when the external conditions are favourable, and incoming air passes through filters. Portable dehumidifiers are available for use as necessary. Heating is provided by a system of warm water welded pipes fitted with water alarms. A separate, more closely controlled and refrigerated store, insulated to avoid drawing in moisture from the adjacent repository, is provided for photographic materials. An Inergen® fire-suppression system is fitted throughout the storage, and a water sprinkler system for the public and staff areas.

The passage leading from the building's main reception towards the search room incorporates exhibition display cases and there is a pleasant sitting-out/tea room for the public, with free Internet access terminals. The search room, with seating for up to 90 readers, is bright, rising through two storeys, and its furnishings very effectively deaden sound. A glazed and sound-proofed bridge passes through the middle of the room at first floor level, linking office functions on either side. In a building where generous space was never going to be a problem, the other main beneficiary is the conservation workshop which, both in terms of floor space and wall height, is all that could be asked for. It has an attendant suite of rooms for document reception, cleaning, isolation if necessary, and sorting. It will clearly set a new benchmark for others to emulate.

More time, and perhaps some tweaking of the control systems and equipment, is needed to bring the internal summer temperature in the repository into line with BS 5454. Conditions in the staff offices can be too cold in winter and too hot in summer, which may be a particular challenge in this kind of building. Overall, however, this appears to have been a strikingly successful and cost-effective scheme with stylish results. It should provide about 20 years of accrual space for the county's archives.

Architects: Devon Property Practice.
Specialist design advisers: Ove Arup and partners.
Cost: approximately £5 million, of which the county council contributed £1.75m and the HLF £3.25m.

English Heritage: National Monuments Record

Kemble Drive, Swindon

Purpose-built 1993 (See Appendix for plan)

Historic GWR offices next to Swindon railway station were converted into offices, storage and public search facilities for the then Royal Commission on the Historical Monuments of England (now part of English Heritage), and this separate but linked purpose-built block was constructed for archive storage: principally for photographs of which there are some 10 million, but with some provision also for archives on paper. After more than a decade, this is still deservedly the flagship photographic archive in the UK.

The storage comprises two linked four-storey modules, with space and pre-laid foundations to accommodate a third module in the future. The complex plant required to maintain a stable environment that is both cool and dry is housed on all four floors, (a) between the two existing modules and (b) on the exposed end which will ultimately adjoin the third module. Ground, first and second floors are devoted to the storage of photographs, and the third

floor to archives on paper, which require less stringent environmental controls.

The construction is of concrete blocks on a reinforced concrete frame, well insulated and with an air cavity, and faced externally with patterned brick for the lower storeys, aluminium cladding for the upper, and bands of insulated glass between the modules (mainly ornamental as the storage has no windows). Ceilings are of coffered concrete, which was cast in situ. The roof, with a generous overhang beyond the walls, is of coated stainless steel. A transparent glazed link, which includes bridges at two levels to provide covered access for trolleys, joins the repository block to the main building while preserving a certain aesthetic detachment.

Great care has been taken with both building and engineering techniques to ensure that a stable and clean environment is maintained for photographic storage. There are back-up systems for all essential components of the plant, with round-the-clock monitoring,

and call-out if necessary. On the side of the building exposed to the sun, an acclimatised circulation corridor separates the building's outer wall from that of the repositories. Despite the significant difference between outdoor and indoor environmental conditions, condensation has not been a problem. Air-conditioning is controlled by a computerised BMS, and the set points for temperature and RH can be separately controlled for separate storage rooms. The air handling system delivers 12-15 air changes per hour with a 10% intake of fresh air. Photographs are stored at set points of 8°C and 32% RH, plans at 12°C and 45% RH, and paper at 16°C and 45% RH. In order to avoid damage from a too rapid transition between storage and consultation environments, photographs undergo overnight (16-hour) acclimatisation before being produced in the reading room for study and again before being returned to storage. For this purpose, on two floors, Swedish-designed double-sided acclimatisation chambers form part of the wall separating the repository from the link to the main building. Air is filtered on intake, clearly very efficiently because despite the site's being located next to busy railway lines diesel fumes do not penetrate the repository nor is any frequent cleaning required to control dust. Internal lighting is u/v filtered

and is set to switch off automatically after a short period if the room is unoccupied.

Fire control strategy relies on smoke and ionisation detectors, a 24-hour security presence on site, and the fact that in an emergency the doors are in effect sealed by the positive pressure maintained by the air-conditioning system, and air can be sucked out to deprive a fire of oxygen. Nitrate film is stored in small rooms each with 4-hour fire resistance and separated from each other by voids so that no two stores are contiguous.

The now mature landscaping has provided a pleasant sitting area between the repository and the staff car park.

Cost: c.£4.6 million (for the archive storage block and its fixtures, fittings and acclimatisation, but not counting concurrent refurbishment to the main building), of which RCHME contributed about two-thirds and the site landlords one-third as part of a public/private partnership.

Architect: DY Davies
Engineers: Ove Arup
Storage: 16 km.
Published references: *The Architects' Journal*, 19 June 1994, pp.17-19. *Museum Practice*, March 1996, pp. 60-2.

Essex Record Office
Wharf Road, Chelmsford

Purpose-built 1999

When Essex County Council first earmarked this brown-field site, adjacent to a gas works, as a possible location for its new record office, the wider plan was to develop the whole area as a cultural district. In the event, the record office was the only part of that plan to be realised, and at the time of writing it still sits in splendid isolation. The site presented a number of hazards, including possible land contamination and flooding from two nearby watercourses, but when detailed assessments had concluded that the risks were acceptably low or containable, building went ahead.

Viewed from the riverside, the building is striking. Its functional segregation into (a) public areas, (b) staff offices and (c) repository is at once visible from the distinctive architectural styles and building materials used for each. The glazed public entrance is inviting, set into a brilliant white façade with the record office's logo emblazoned in silver, and indeed the exterior aspect of all the public functions is full of visual interest. The roof line sweeps boldly upwards, and on one side giant baffles block out direct sunlight from the search room. In deliberate contrast, the repository is faced in brick, and one of its walls tucks into the public entrance. The elongated block to the rear, for staff offices, appears by contrast almost too starkly functional.

The record office was designed and equipped to the highest specification, in line with BS 5454. The repository, built on a steel frame with concrete infilling, and clad in ivory coloured brick with dark blue banding, is of three storeys, each divided into two main strongrooms, and with smaller rooms on one floor for photographic and magnetic media. It is windowless and of heavy mass to achieve high thermal inertia and minimise the need for mechanical intervention to control the environment. It is, nevertheless, fully air-conditioned. An automated Argonite® fire-suppression system is installed, with smoke and heat detection and alarm systems. The two-hour fire doors of the repositories are

supplemented by steel roller doors offering a further two-hours protection. The roof, which houses the plant room, is unusual among recent archive buildings in not extending beyond the line of the repository walls. Technical facilities include reprographics and digitisation studios, sound recording facilities and a conservation workshop.

Generous space on the ground floor has been allocated to public services, which include a pleasant reception-cum-exhibition area, a well equipped lecture theatre and an education room. Dedicated space is also provided in the building for the research centre of the Essex Society for Family History and for the Victoria County History. The search room, situated on the first floor, with seating for up to 120 readers, is among the largest and best equipped in the country. To minimise noise and disturbance it is divided by glazed partitions into separate zones for reception, and for the consultation respectively of microforms, local studies reference works, original archival documents, maps and large documents, and

audio-visual archives. It is generously provided with computer terminals for access to the electronic catalogue. Here and in the foyer below, an electronic sign board indicates when readers' documents are ready for collection.

After only five years of occupancy, the rate of use of some of the room spaces and facilities has already changed significantly compared with initial estimates, and the allocation of space between functions is being re-thought.

Architects: W S Atkins.
Cost: *c.* £10.5 million excluding the site.
Funded by Essex County Council.
Published references: 'Tomorrow comes at last', in *Essex Record Office Update*, no. 35 (summer 2000).

FILM ARCHIVES

Some film is held in many of the buildings covered by this study. Among the more specialised facilities, the *National Screen and Sound Archive of Wales* is noted briefly in the case study for the National Library of Wales, and the *East Anglia Film Archive* in that for Norfolk Record Office and East Anglia Film Archive. In the photographic field the *English Heritage National Monuments Record* is also featured. The following are among the new developments in the provision of specialist accommodation for film archives in this period.

Northern Region Film and Television Archive

University of Teesside, Middlesbrough.
Purpose-built storage and newly equipped technical facilities, 2004

The holdings of the NRFTA (estd 1998) are split between this site and Tyne and Wear Archives in Newcastle. The storage at Teesside was made possible by a major grant from the EU Strategic Development budget, together with funding from the University, Gateshead council, Northern Film and Media and commercial sponsors. Whilst arrangements can be made to view films on both sites no dedicated public search facilities have been provided here, in anticipation of future access being largely online.

The windowless, single storey building is of reinforced concrete internally, faced with brick externally, with an insulated cavity. The storage is air-conditioned throughout, the air being cleaned and filtered on intake. Separate air handling units in each of four storage vaults allow different conditions to be maintained for acetate film and magnetic sound tracks; black and white film and polyester-based magnetic

tape; and masters. An acclimatisation area is provided for material in transit from storage to consultation and back. Fire protection is by means of an automatic Inergen® system.

Cost: £780,000.
The Archive's website (www.nrfta.org.uk) includes further information and photographs.

North West Film Archive

Manchester Metropolitan University.
Converted part of former warehouse, 1996

Even after a decade of operation, this is still in many respects a state-of-the art facility. NWFA had moved into the upper part of this Georgian former warehouse as early as 1985, but in the 1990s the lower floors and open-air loading bay were cleared and gutted and new premises were in effect purpose-built within the old shell. The main shell is of red brick. A new enclosed entrance in concrete and glass with metal-framed windows leads into a spacious reception area rising at the front through two storeys, with a polished wooden floor. To right and left are staff offices, separated from the reception area by glazed doors and windows which give depth of vision even to the more confined spaces. Behind the reception area is a large viewing room which also houses a collection of historic cameras and film equipment.

A spiral staircase from the reception area leads to a mezzanine office deck and a film conservation, processing and copying suite. To the rear at this level is a suite of 6 storage rooms for the film archive. These are segregated from the rest of the building by a fire wall of concrete blockwork, and further protected by a smoke detection and alarm system and an automatic Inergen® system. Each room has a metal ceiling, above which is a waterproof membrane to prevent water ingress from the floors above (which are not occupied by NWFA). Temperature and relative humidity are individually controlled, respectively for colour film; black and white film; magnetic media; and paper. Films are allowed to acclimatise gradually, by being moved from one room to the next in the appropriate sequence, culminating in a small acclimatisation room, before being made available for consultation. An isolation room is also provided, fitted with extractor fans, for the storage of any film affected by 'vinegar syndrome'.

Architects: Mills, Beaumont, Leavy, Channon. Cost: c.£1 million, funded by the University, with additional support for equipment from the HLF in a second phase.

Yorkshire Film Archive

Fountains Learning Centre, College of York St John, York.

Purpose-built, 2003

In the Centre's foyer, plasma screens show film clips to advertise the Archive, which was funded by the HLF and the regional development agency at a cost of £700,000. Direct on-site access facilities are modest but well-appointed: the viewing room, with lighting recessed into the ceiling to avoid glare, can accommodate three readers at individual screens equipped with headphones, or up to ten to view films on a wall-mounted screen. For staff and technical services, separate rooms are provided for the director, acquisition/editing, preservation/repair, collection management, and education.

The four, windowless air-conditioned storage vaults are built on a frame of steel and concrete blocks, faced externally with brick and stone. Videotape is stored at 15°C + 1°C and 40-45% RH, and film at 10°C + 1°C and 30-35% RH, with vigorous air circulation. Conditions are monitored constantly through a BMS. An automatic gas fire-suppression system is fitted. No nitrate stock is held.

Glasgow University Library Special Collections
Hillhead Street, Glasgow

Purpose-built extension above existing building, 1997

The main multi-storey block of Glasgow University Library dates from 1968, with supporting, higher-standing 'Tuscan' towers at intervals around the perimeter. Special Collections used to be housed in the basement and on the ground floor (now levels 2 and 3 respectively), but a possible upward extension was provided for by the architect from the start, and this indeed is how the department was eventually re-housed, on a new level 12 added in 1997.

Unlike for example France, the United Kingdom has few examples of archives and manuscripts housed in tower blocks. The risks involved in accommodating them at the top of such a building include those from a fire arising on the floors below, and from the exposure of the roof and fabric to the weather, and in particular to strong winds. But these have been systematically countered here: the extension is built on a load-bearing and fireproof steel base over a 15cm concrete slab, and the distinctive parabola roof is fitted with air deflectors to help resist the onslaught of strong winds. The roof itself is of lightweight (Kalzip) ribbed aluminium sheeting with two layers of insulation below, whilst the external walls of the new extension are protected by a layer of low-maintenance (Eternit) rainscreen cladding which is separated from the structural walls by a cavity.

The public entrance to the new accommodation is through a lobby area with

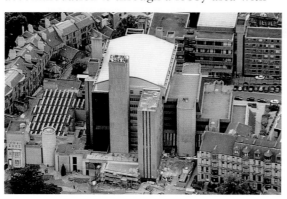

a display unit set into one wall to allow some of the department's treasures to be made more visible. From here, a corridor with large outer windows of filtered glass, provides plenty of natural north light for the reading room through a second bank of internal windows opposite. The reading room itself, with distinctive, elegantly designed wooden furniture, has a sloping roof and uplighting from a rank of 9 luminaires. It can seat about two dozen readers in comfort.

The fully air-conditioned stack (strongroom) accommodates printed books, theses, manuscripts and archives, at $18°C \pm 1°$ and 55% RH $\pm 5\%$. Three of its walls are external, whilst the fourth adjoins the reading room and adjacent Henry Heaney seminar room which can accommodate 50. Set into one of the outer walls of the stack are three windows, protected by light-excluding blinds. The windows can be opened should the plant fail or additional ventilation be required. Plant is housed partly in one of the perimeter towers, and partly in the roof void, which is tanked, externally drained and fitted with water alarms.

The racking is mostly mobile, and an impressive 3 metres high. It is set into a raised floor equipped with adjustable jacks to correct any deflection, and no problems have been experienced to date. A generous metre-wide walkway has been left all round the outer edges of the racking.

A separate room with RH controlled to a lower level is set aside for photographs, but the heat from its own dehumidifier tends to make it warmer than is ideal. Staff offices are located in one of the adjacent perimeter towers.

Architects: Holmes Partnership.
Cost: *c.*£4 million including redevelopment of the main entrance on the ground floor of which £2m came from a SHEFC grant. No separate figures available for Special Collections.
Storage capacity: *c.*10 km.
Photograph courtesy of Glasgow University

Gloucestershire Record Office extension

Purpose-built pods inside warehouse structure,
1997-1999

The core of the present record office is a converted school to which, in successive phases of development, various extensions have been added and modifications made. Outside, the visual impression is drab, and even somewhat intimidating, with barbed wire on the perimeter wall to dissuade intruders. But inside, despite the rather motley collection of buildings and rooms, it now provides comfortable and well equipped facilities for both public and staff. It is featured here not on account of this parent building or of its general ambience, but for its modular storage system, which is unique in the UK.

Faced in the late 1990s with the need for a further expansion of the archive storage accommodation, the County Council acquired an adjacent property: a warehouse with walls of brick and corrugated steel and a saw-toothed roof of corrugated steel panels carried on a metal frame. This had formerly been a car repair workshop, but had lain vacant for a number of years.

The warehouse itself was not of sufficiently robust construction to be seen as a candidate for conversion into an archive repository in its own right. But it was fundamentally in good condition. So the warehouse structure was retained as an outer canopy or shell and then, as resources permitted, a series of modular storage 'pods' was built within it, standing completely free of the outer structure. The County Council bought the warehouse and paid for the first two pods and for a covered walkway to link the warehouse to the rest of the record office. Over the next two years, with the help of major grants from the HLF (which also covered significant upgrading of the existing school buildings), further pods were added, bringing the total to nine of which one (half-size) is reserved for the storage of special media and the remainder are for general archive storage.

As the new accommodation was designed to give expansion space for 20 years in all, it has been possible to rent out some of the surplus space to other public bodies for archive storage on a short-term basis, until such time as it is needed by Gloucestershire. This solution to storage problems arose essentially from local site opportunities that are unlikely to be exactly replicated elsewhere, but it has proved very practical and cost-effective. Most pertinently it provides a secure and very stable storage environment for the archives.

The windowless pod walls are of well insulated concrete block construction, with flat, weatherproof concrete roofs that stand well below the outer (warehouse) roof. Each pod is fitted with mobile racking. For fire safety each pod has two doors. No automatic fire-suppression system is provided but there is a comprehensive detection and alarm system. There is no form of air-conditioning or heating within the warehouse shell, other than in a segregated outer portion which has been developed as a sorting and staff area. With the exception of the special media store, the pods themselves are not air-conditioned, nor is there any mechanical air circulation, although small wall vents and the opening and closing of the doors provide some air change. Warm water pipes, carried fairly low on the inner walls of the pods, allow the temperature to be raised, and each pod is equipped with a portable dehumidifier for use if necessary. By these simple means, some of the most stable environmental conditions anywhere in the UK for archive storage are maintained here, even in extremes of hot and cold weather. The pod for special media has its own air-conditioning unit, sited immediately outside the pod wall (but within the warehouse perimeter).

The only significant problems that have arisen relate to the outer fabric of the warehouse, which requires regular maintenance but is not easily accessible on all sides. Condensation sometimes occurs under the outer roof. But overall this has thus far proved to be a highly cost-effective and energy-efficient strategy.

Architects: W S Atkins.
Storage capacity: 1,564 cu.m.

Guardian and Observer 'Newsroom': archive and visitor centre

Farringdon Road, London EC1

Converted former warehouse, 2002

The Newsroom was commissioned as part of the newspapers' celebration of the Millennium, to provide a new visitor centre with public services and staff offices, just across the road from the main Guardian and Observer offices. It includes an impressive exhibition hall, a lecture theatre and separate large meeting room, an education room, a public search room, archive storage, a small café/deli to encourage passers-by to drop in, and staff offices. As far as the archives are concerned, the present arrangements are, however, temporary, as new purpose-built facilities are at the planning stage as part of the move of Guardian Newspapers Ltd to the King's Cross area in 2008. Even so, excellent facilities of this kind, which have attracted wide acclaim, deserve more than passing mention.

Much of the handsome brick façade of the original bonded warehouse (1875, but adapted to other uses later) and its outer walls, also of brick, have been retained. The inside has been re-modelled, following the general lines of the original building, and there is a new glazed entrance. An existing modern extension at the rear was adapted to provide three levels of meeting rooms and public and staff facilities.

There are several innovative features, designed to make the public spaces as flexible and useful as possible. The raked seating of the lecture theatre can be folded away on movable platforms, and the partition wall separating the lecture theatre from the gallery folded back, to create a large reception space. Movable vertical exhibition panels, normally sited in the centre of the gallery, can be overlaid with additional temporary panels, but can also be stowed away altogether. These are supplemented by free-standing display cases equipped with fibre-optic lighting to cater for changing displays.

The archive storage accommodation consists of two inter-connected rooms, abuttting one of the building's outer walls, but has its own inner wall. The cavity between is insulated. The internal walls are of concrete blockwork and double-skinned plaster board.

The air-conditioning for this area runs off its own dedicated plant. Incoming air is filtered, and cooler, dryer conditions can be maintained in one of the rooms for the storage of photographs. High (3.6m) mobile racking maximises the use of the available storage space. For energy efficiency, the lighting is controlled by movement sensors. Fire protection is by means of an automatic Argonite® gas system.

The school room, which can accommodate 30 students, and the archive search room are both well equipped and comfortable, and look out on to a small garden planted with tall bamboo.

Architects: Allies and Morrison.
Cost: approx. £4 million, funded by the Scott Trust.
Storage: approx. 1.6 km (floor areas: paper store 32 sq m., photo store 28 sq.m.)
Published references: L Dodd, 'A showcase for history', in *The Guardian past and present: Newsroom* (2002), pp.64-9.

Hereford Cathedral Library and Archives

Purpose-built, 1996

This attractive building of red sandstone occupies a strategic site in the streetscape, adjacent to the west end of the cathedral and built on to the medieval cloisters and the 19th century library building adjoining. It succeeds splendidly in blending ancient and modern styles and materials, and was the Royal Fine Art Commission's Building of the Year for 1997.

The building comprises a main, rectangular block set parallel to the west side of the cloisters and a linking block, at right-angles to this, joining it to the cloisters.

The main block is of two lofty storeys and a basement, but has an additional mezzanine level (with lift and WCs) on the main entry staircase. The reading room for the cathedral's library and archives is on the upper floor,

beneath the exposed oak timbers of the steeply pitched roof, and with oak furniture and flooring and cedar panelling to match. On a sunny day it is light and airy, although in the winter natural light from the elegant windows is sometimes at a premium. Much of the library is on open access here, in the linking block at the same level, and in the 19th century range beyond, which also houses the staff offices.

Below the main part of the reading room is the new accommodation for the cathedral's famous chained library. Between this and the cloisters is the climatised chamber housing the Hereford Mappa Mundi in a display case with subdued lighting as it is on continuous public display.

The strongroom for archives and rare books is below ground level. Its walls are of concrete blockwork, protected on the outside by a waterproof membrane. The room is fitted with mobile racking and is fully air-conditioned to BS 5454 standard and protected by an Argonite® fire-suppression system which also serves the chained library and the Mappa chamber. Natural climatisation methods were considered for the chained library and Mappa chamber, but to ensure environmental stability air-conditioning was introduced.

Architect: William Whitfield.
Cost: approximately £2.2 million. External funding came from the National Heritage Memorial Fund and JP Getty.
Published references: J Tiller, 'The new library building', in *Hereford cathedral. A history*, ed G Aylmer and J Tiller (2000)

Leicestershire, Leicester and Rutland (Record Office for)

Wigston Magna, Leicester

Converted school with purpose-built repository,
1993 (with some remedial work 2003) (See
Appendix for plan)

This building, situated three and a half miles
from the centre of Leicester, was funded by
Leicestershire County Council prior to the local
government reorganisation of 1997 which led
to the creation of the joint archive service for
the three authorities. It was opened at the very
beginning of the period covered by the present
volume, but still deserves a place here as a good
example of a cost-effective and relatively simple
conversion. Both the conversion and the new
build took inspiration from the very similar
site at the Suffolk Record Office, Ipswich (see
ABUK1).

From the street frontage, all that is visible is
the red brick former school building of 1881,
spruced up, completely re-roofed and given
a new canopied public entrance. This now
houses the public services and staff offices. A
detached 1930s building in the grounds to the
rear, which housed the art and domestic science
departments, was retained and converted into a
conservation workshop. As these buildings had
been vacant for a number of years and had become dilapidated it was perhaps inevitable that
a certain amount of deep-seated damp in the
internal walls should emerge only after occupancy, but this has not been a major problem.

As with all conversions, the existing
structure and the layout of rooms imposed
some constraints. Many of the original
schoolrooms and features were simply retained,
re-painted and given new furnishings. In the
public areas, which include separate rooms for
the consultation of microforms and original

documents, the results are bright and generally comfortable, although the document search room which has west facing windows tends to suffer from solar gain in hot summers. The existing room layout also largely determined that staff offices would have to be placed to the side of the search room, which results in a lot of traffic through this space. Despite these inconveniences, this is still an eminently serviceable building. It was designed with a certain amount of flexibility, for example with a sliding partition wall between two of the public areas so that they can be opened up into one for exhibitions and events. And in other respects it has proved sufficiently adaptable to changing needs including that for increased electronic (including Internet) access. The allocation of functions to some ancillary rooms has also changed somewhat with time and changing demands.

The two-storey repository block was purpose-built on the former school playground. It is linked to the main building at one end. An external glazed corridor runs along it, joining the staff and public facilities in the original school building to the conservation workshop. The repository (of concrete construction on a steel frame) is attractively faced in cream and red brick with blue banding. As at Ipswich, the repository was initially designed with heavy mass and insulation to deliver stable environmental conditions without significant mechanical intervention. Heating and dehumidification were provided as part of the original design. When the early indications

were that these measures would not prove sufficient in a hot summer, chillers were added to the outside of the repository block and fan-assisted air-circulation inside, and with their help environmental conditions have since remained both stable and closely controllable within BS 5454 without a full air-conditioning system.

With the building fully loaded, mobile racking on the upper floor began to roll of its own accord under the weight of the documents. It took several anxious years to determine responsibility for putting this right and then to develop a solution which was relatively straightforward but costly. Some documents on the first floor were temporarily moved in 2003 while the racking was adapted *in situ* to carry electric motors which restrain any unwanted movement in addition to making the racking easier to move. At the same time a further improvement was made to the stability of the repository by adding metal braces to the internal walls on both floors, against any risk of movement in strong winds. These remedies appear to have been entirely effective. Although it was designed with capacity for about thirteen years, the repository now looks as if it will serve for at least fifteen before additional storage space is required, either here or elsewhere.

Architects: ADW partnership.
Cost: £1.6 million excluding the site, which was already owned by the County Council.
Storage: 1,300 cu.m.

London Metropolitan Archives extension

Northampton Road, London EC1

Purpose-built, 1993

London Metropolitan Archives is by far the largest local authority archive service in the United Kingdom, and in terms of storage capacity its buildings are in a league of their own, ranking with the large national repositories. The Greater London Record Office (as it then was) first occupied this Clerkenwell site in 1982, moving into a converted printing works. Those original premises were themselves being significantly upgraded at the time of this study, in a phased programme lasting several years, to improve the storage environment for archives and to provide space, among other things, for the modern records management programme of the Corporation of London. Following recent re-structuring, the Corporation now runs a joint archive service that embraces the earlier, county-wide LMA service and the archives of the Corporation itself.

The 1993 extension described here was fitted into the space between the printing works and Northampton Road. A tall, brick-clad building with purely ornamental 'bay windows' to soften the appearance (in this residential area) of the repository's vast external wall, it is linked by a glazed bridge to the original building. There are three floors above ground and one below, all devoted purely to storage since the other record office functions are housed in the original building. The combination of a high thermal inertia design and full air-conditioning has provided stable environmental conditions throughout, in line with BS 5454. The plant room is housed in the (tanked) roof space, behind louvred vents, and has water alarms. The ceiling of the floor below is insulated and further protected by a vapour barrier. The roof itself comprises inner and outer layers of metal profiled decking separated by rockwool insulation.

The building was originally fitted with a halon automatic fire-suppression system. This has recently been replaced not with a different kind of gaseous system but with water sprinklers, as in the original building. That decision was taken in part because the pipework for the sprinklers required less interference with the basic fabric of the building which was

contributing so meaningfully to the overall environmental stability of the storage areas. A large water tank was installed at the side of the car park to feed the system should the mains themselves prove inadequate.

Each floor is divided into two compartments to assist environmental and fire control. The entrances on each floor are protected by a double airlock, beyond which the fire doors are additionally fitted with steel roller screens that can be automatically deployed in an emergency. This applies also to the doors between compartments. There is an aspirating fire alarm system. As a result of an engineering research project conducted by City University, a system of 'power factor correction' was introduced to ensure that energy is efficiently used throughout the building and that equipment,

lighting and plant are turned off when not required. The air-handling system works on a ratio of 20% fresh air, filtered on intake, to 80% recycled air.

Tall mobile racking is installed throughout, and in the basement the units are 4.9 metres high, making them the tallest used for regular archive storage in the UK (although some automated retrieval systems elsewhere, for example for deeds and film storage, are considerably higher).

In design terms, this simply-stated building without flamboyant features has proved an excellent investment.

Architects: Culpin Partnership.
Cost: £3.859 million.
Storage: 34 km (2,500 sq.m).

National Archives of Scotland Thomas Thomson House

Edinburgh

Purpose-built, 1995 (See Appendix for plan)

Unusually among the case studies in this volume, Thomas Thomson House, built on a 'brown-field' site in the western suburbs of Edinburgh, is an archive building with no public services. These continue to be provided in central Edinburgh, whilst Thomas Thomson House (NAS's third repository, after General Register House and West Register House) is restricted to archive storage, conservation and document processing facilities and staff offices. On this basis a simple, T-shaped design, was a natural choice. The site is well demarcated, with its own perimeter fence.

The two blocks are very different in concept and appearance. The storage block, of three storeys each having three main compartments – capable of further subdivision, as on the ground floor for high security and special media – is windowless, and of heavy mass in order to achieve high thermal inertia and energy efficiency. It has insulated and ventilated wall and roof cavities. The building was specified to be of a high quality, to meet BS 5454 and be sufficiently robust to last for 125 years. The steel and concrete frame is clad externally with large pre-fabricated panels of brick, which on the long wall at the rear are fitted with louvred smoke extract vents for use in an emergency. The roof, of Swedish manufacture, covered with continuously welded stainless steel, curves elegantly over the repository, with a generous overhang to protect the walls. The repositories are air-conditioned throughout, with most of the plant situated in the corridors outside the rooms, and in a storage tower which fills the angle between the two blocks. A computerised BMS monitors the air-conditioning, and the environment in each storage compartment can be controlled independently to achieve different conditions for different media. A dry-pipe automatic water sprinkler system, fed from a gargantuan tank below ground, is at the heart of the fire-protection strategy. An innovative siphoning drainage system intended to take run-off from the large roof has not functioned efficiently and is being replaced by more conventional methods.

By contrast, viewed from the north, the administrative and technical block is a mass of shimmering glass, reflecting both the surroundings and the changing colours of the sky. This guarantees generous natural light for the (north-facing) conservation workshop, purpose-designed by conservators and still after ten years serving very well, although a less welcome effect of the ample fenestration is a reduction in the amount of wall space. Unlike the storage, this block is not air-conditioned, but is heated as necessary and equipped with openable windows so that staff have a degree of control over their working conditions. Document reception and processing are well served, with spacious rooms. The south-facing rooms to the rear have much less fenestration,

but a spinal corridor rising through the full height of the building admits daylight via the roof.

With the growth in demand for computer services and in particular digitisation, a room originally designated for temporary storage of documents during processing has been converted into a digitisation studio. At the time of writing an extension was under consideration which could eventually bring not only additional storage space but also public services to this site.

Architects: Building Design Partnership.
Storage capacity: approximately 42 km (not yet fully racked).
Cost: including fitting out, £11.2 million.
Published reference: G MacKenzie and L Ramsay, 'An integrated approach to preservation: the new Scottish Record Office building in Edinburgh,' in *La conservation: une science en évolution* (ARSAG, Paris, 1997 [ISSN 0765-0248], pp.36-43). P Anderson, 'Thomas Thomson House – five years on', in *Atlanti* 11 no 2 (2001), pp.158-67

National Library of Wales

Aberystwyth

Third library building: purpose-built, 1996
Reading room: in situ conversion, 2004
Visitor experience (in situ conversion)
and Drwm auditorium (new build), 2004

The period under review has seen a number of important developments with regard to archives and manuscripts at the National Library of Wales, and also further important improvements to the Library's exhibition, meeting and visitor facilities from which archives and manuscripts have benefited.

The Library's third building, opened by The Queen in 1996, was constructed at the rear of this hill-top site. It is joined on to the earlier buildings in such a way as to be invisible from the Library's main drive, but from the south side, (and even when viewed from a distance in the train) the visitor can get a good impression of the ensemble of the buildings, and the blend is impressive. The third building, of concrete construction clad externally in brick and reconstituted stone, is on six levels (including ground and lower ground). The top five are devoted to the storage of books and maps and are protected by a water sprinkler system. The lowest level, which is only partly basement, following the slope of the land, provides 20 storage rooms for archives and manuscripts, 10 either side of a spinal corridor. Three of these, however, are interconnected and lined with copper to serve as a Faraday Cage to protect

magnetic media from interference. This is the only such facility encountered in this survey. The ceiling above the entire lower ground floor has been constructed of concrete strong enough in principle to withstand the collapse of the whole building above. At this level, fire-suppression is by means of an automatic carbon dioxide system. The climatic conditions in the rooms can be individually controlled to allow, for example, cooler and drier storage for microfilm masters.

Back in the main building, a new reading room for archives, manuscripts, maps and rare books was constructed in rooms formerly used for library storage on the south side of the building. The public enter this long and impressively large space at the centre, where there is a concave reception desk to draw them in. To the right, behind an engraved glass partition and through a security gate, is the main area for consultation of original materials, with ample up-lighting from suspended lamps. A number of computer terminals provide access to the electronic catalogues and to the Internet (a facility also available in a new, comfortable sitting-out area for readers just outside the reading room door). A range of staff offices has been positioned along the south side, looking into the reading area. At the other end of the reading room, and mostly under more subdued (dimmable) lighting, are seats for the consultation of microform surrogate materials. At intervals throughout both halves of the room the height of some of the tables is adjustable at the touch of a button to suit the needs of individual readers. This south-facing room inevitably tends to get hot in summer, when portable air-conditioning units are provided as necessary.

Among other notable developments, funded with the aid of a £2.4 million grant from the HLF, are a Visitor Experience including new exhibition display cases; and the Drwm (drum), a structure clad in polished stainless steel, designed by Partneriaeth James Jenkins, and created inside a covered former courtyard, to house a 100-seat auditorium/theatre for the National Screen and Sound Archive of Wales and for more general use by the Library. This facility can be made accessible when the Library is closed and can be hired for private use. Above the auditorium is housed the new Hengwrt exhibition gallery where the Library's treasures can be displayed in a secure climate-controlled environment.

Published references:'Take a virtual tour round the National Library of Wales' in *Ecclesiastical & Heritage World*, 13 (2002), p.7. The official opening of the third library building of the National Library of Wales (brochure, 1996). C Kitching, 'Preservation in new buildings', in *LIBER Quarterly* 10, no 3, (2000), pp. 376-86.
Photo: National Library of Wales

Norfolk Record Office and East Anglia Film Archive

The Archive Centre, Norwich

(Norfolk County Council/University of East Anglia)

Purpose-built, 2003 (See Appendix for plan)

After the disastrous fire at Norwich Central Library in 1994 where it was then housed, Norfolk Record Office had to move to temporary quarters elsewhere in the city while planning took place for a new permanent home. A partnership with the university was discussed, and a site on its campus was initially explored but eventually ruled out. Instead, the idea was developed of building a new archive centre for the two partners in the grounds of County Hall on the outskirts of the city. The absence of significant space constraints provided an excellent footprint for the Centre whilst still leaving a generous setting of fields and woodland. The lie of the land was awkward only to the extent that it was necessary to have steps down into the Centre, and hence a lift for disabled access at the entrance.

The segregation of functions is immediately clear in the design and layout: the new building comprises a two-storey block for public and technical services and staff offices, linked to a three-storey repository block. The building's horizontal axis is long, as becomes clear from the visitor's first view of the interior along an impressive exhibition gallery leading from the front door to the readers' reception counter at the far end. Facilities in the gallery include a plasma screen for showing film and other digital images. Public cloakrooms, a public common room and the education and meeting rooms are situated near the front entrance, so that these and the exhibition gallery itself can be used at times when the research facilities are closed.

The record office has a single large search room, with separate zones for the study respectively of archives, finding aids and microforms, the latter in a darker (windowless) area. At one end, two sound-proofed partitions separate off a small control room and study area for the Norfolk Sound Archive. In the main reading room the height of some of the chairs and tables is adjustable to suit the needs

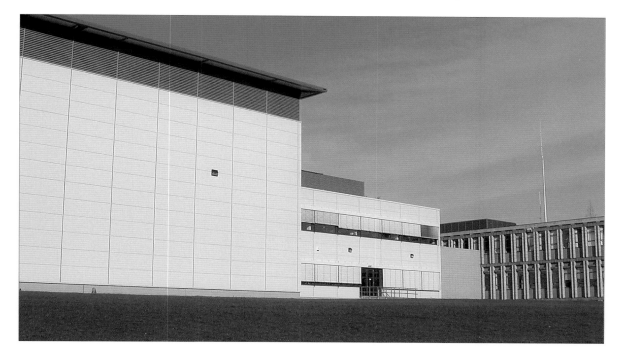

of different users (and different documents), and with the same eye to flexibility the main meeting room, the Green Room, has tables with castors and brakes, and with tiltable tops for stacking. The East Anglian Film Archive (EAFA) has its own viewing room, with appropriately relaxed, comfortable furniture.

The repository block provides three floors of archive storage. The ground floor is divided in two, each partner occupying half the space, whilst the two upper floors are allocated to the record office. The walls are of heavy mass and insulation, to do much of the work of stabilising the environment, but full air-conditioning is provided in order to maintain conditions in accordance with BS 5454. In

the record office's accommodation large pneumatic fans mounted on the ceiling ensure good air circulation. Plant is mainly located in a detached building to the rear. Conditions are monitored by a BMS and also by wireless data-loggers. An automatic Argonite® fire-suppression system is provided. The storage accommodation for EAFA comprises two rooms for black and white film, one for video, and a cooler one for colour film, with an adjacent acclimatisation room. Different climatic conditions are provided to suit the respective media. After some initial difficulties the environment even in the coolest room now appears to have settled down. A small detached building houses nitrate stock.

Technical facilities include film processing rooms for EAFA, whilst the Record Office has a suite of interlinked rooms for reception, isolation, cleaning and boxing, plus a well-equipped conservation workshop which includes a tanked and slightly sloping floor to ensure the containment and drainage of any spillage.

Architects: in-house, with advice from David Bernstein. Cost: £6.7 million, of which £4.2 m was provided by the HLF, £2.2 m by the county council and £0.3 m by the university.
Record office storage capacity: 5,800 sq.m.

Orkney Library and Archives
Kirkwall

Purpose-built 2003 (See Appendix for plan)

Orkney's library service is at least arguably the oldest in Scotland having been founded in 1683. Its archive service, established in 1973, was the first local authority archive service to be set up anywhere in Scotland outside the main cities. With this striking new two-storey building, which occupies the site of the former auction mart, Orkney continues to set the pace. As well as the library (including, in the Orkney Room, an extensive local studies section) and the archives, the building houses the Biodiversity Records Centre, Orkney's Talking Newspaper and the Family History Society. A conference/exhibition room and other meeting rooms are also provided.

Externally, the overall style owes something to Arts and Crafts. Its gables reflect traditional vernacular building style, but at the same time the materials chosen have a more modern look and colour, with a distinctive facing of light render and polished blockwork. As originally conceived the building was differently orientated, with most of the archival functions located on the north side away from exposure to the sun. When, for planning reasons, the site eventually available for development was more constrained than expected the footprint had to be swung round by 90 degrees. A plan to use mainly natural ventilation then had to be revised in favour of mechanical support. The adjacent land is prone to seasonal flooding in extreme weather, and to protect against this the ground floor is raised a little from the surrounds, whilst all the archival functions apart from the loading bay (within an enclosed garage) and document reception area are located on the first floor.

The building, on a steel frame, has 100 mm concrete blockwork on the exterior, 100 mm insulated cavity, and then a further 150 mm of blockwork to ensure high thermal inertia. Both floors are of concrete, with a high floor-loading capability to support mobile racking. The upper floor is carried on steel beams. The roof

space includes thick insulation and externally the pitched roof, on a steel frame, is clad in slate. Air-conditioning is provided by a separate unit in each of the four archive storage areas, and these can be set to different requirements in accordance with BS 5454.

The archive search room can seat around a dozen readers in comfort, with additional seat-ing for those consulting maps and microfilm. There are also two carrels for those wishing to consult sound archives. Technical facilities include a suite of rooms for reprographics.

Architect: Laurie Sparrow.
Cost: £4 million for the whole building.
Storage capacity: 208 cu.m.

Oxfordshire Record Office

Cowley, Oxford

Converted church, 2000 (See Appendix for plan)

This is surely the only record office bearing an inscription on the exterior: *Peace be within thy walls*! St Luke's, Cowley (1937), a sturdy building of sand-coloured brick, had by the late 1990s been redundant for a number of years. The diocese agreed to release it to the County Council for this new purpose subject to an undertaking not to make irreversible changes to the main structure. The building has, however, been tastefully and significantly enlarged by the addition of long lean-to glasshouses beyond the outer walls of the original aisles. That on the north side (the left as viewed from the street) houses the public entrance. It is pleasantly appointed, with refreshment facilities, display space, WCs, and lockers for coats and bags. That on the south side houses the conservation workshop, which has been nicely fitted out with purpose-designed furniture finished in light blue. The glass in the sloping roofs of both extensions is tinted to minimise the effects of direct sunlight, but this can still be an issue on sunny days for the short period when the sun is directly on the conservation workshop, or indeed for the longer period when it is warming up the reception area.

From reception, readers pass through an exhibition room created out of a former chapel, into the main search room which occupies the chancel. This light and airy space has created a friendly working environment for staff and readers, with seating for around 50. The old reredos is preserved in situ, as is most of the original painted decoration and some of the internal woodwork. The space on the south side formerly occupied by the organ has been divided into two levels, the lower one housing a microform reading room and the upper one the county archivist's office, which directly overlooks the search room. An education room,

staff room and staff WCs and shower occupy the remainder of the ground floor at the east end.

In what was the church's nave, a free-standing insulated concrete box has been constructed to house three floors of storage. This is carried on its own steel frame, with all the uprights and cross beams protected by fire retardant casing. The frame itself, together with the church's original stone pillars which remain in situ, of course impose some constraints on the free use of the space for storage. They have been well worked around in planning the conversion, but all the racking had to be specially made to fit the particular context. An FM200® gas suppression system is installed, together with full air-conditioning, and the environment is maintained within BS 5454 parameters. Much of the air-handling plant sits on the church's roofs, protected from pigeons by netting. On the top floor, storage accounts for only half the space, the remainder being devoted to staff offices. Here, the tops of the original nave aisle arches have been incorporated as features, decorated with inscriptions in a millennium project by the Oxford Scribes, the words being taken from some of the archives themselves.

Given a building which is itself of some architectural merit and in good physical condition, conversions of this kind can be a viable solution to the challenges of storage and access, and in Oxfordshire's case this has been money well spent.

Architects: WS Atkins
Storage: c.6 miles.
Cost: £3.5 million including £2.25 m from HLF and £0.45 m from Oxford diocese.

Perth and Kinross Council Archives

AK Bell Library, Perth

Purpose-built within library, 1994

The AK Bell Library, with self-contained archives department, was built as an extension to an elegant Victorian stone building which had originally housed Perth Infirmary but had since had a number of other uses. The new-build, much of it faced in matching stone, nicely complements the old, and the new west wing, which houses the archives on the first floor, above the public auditorium, is designed in a homogeneous classical style. A third of the funding came from the Gannochy Trust and the project was carried out by Perth & Kinross Recreational Facilities Ltd (subsequently Perth & Kinross Leisure), from which the Council now rents the building.

The public search room is entered from the main library's reference section and seats up to 10 readers. Off it, separated by a glazed wall and door, is a single staff office. Staff access to the storage accommodation is in turn situated directly off the search room, the perimeter of the storage being defined by a concrete-block fire wall. The entire storage space is windowless. It has outer walls on three sides and here the cavity between the

concrete blocks and the outer stone facing is insulated. A concrete floor separates the archive from the auditorium below. Whilst the floor loading was not rated strong enough to take mobile racking, good use has been made of the strongroom's generous height (rising right up to the pitched roof, with no false ceiling) to provide a mezzanine floor with a steel-mesh walkway, carried on a steel frame. The static metal racking rises through the full height of the two levels, and is configured in such a way as to allow generous walking space around the perimeter of the racking as well as within the aisles. A double-skinned metal roof with insulation between the two layers tops the building. After a disappointing start, in which the installation of a full air-conditioning system was postponed for budgetary reasons, the necessary equipment was eventually acquired. It continues to perform reasonably well, within BS 5454 recommendations. Fire and intruder alarms are linked to the respective emergency services.

A number of design faults just take the edge off an otherwise good example of a small archive building. Service pipes pass through the storage; and despite many remedial efforts over a decade a minor water leak still occasionally troubles one perimeter walkway of the strongroom. The storage accommodation is now nearly full, and the staff quarters feel cramped and constricted when compared with others examined in the course of this study. Nevertheless, the accommodation for the archives department here is a model of compactness, simplicity of design, and fitness for purpose for a local authority archive of medium size.

Architect: in-house.
Cost: overall cost of Library over £6 million; no separate figures for archives.
Storage: *c*.1.5 km.
Published reference: 'The AK Bell Library', in D Harrison (ed), *Library buildings in the United Kingdom 1990-1994* (1995), pp.221-4.

St George's Chapel Archives and Chapter Library

Windsor

Converted 15th-century undercroft, 1999

Before this new development, the archives of St George's Chapel Windsor were housed in the ancient Treasury, the 'Aerary', but some also in unsuitable, unclimatised conditions in the chapel's Schorn Tower where working conditions for staff were difficult and the tasks of sorting and listing the archives, producing them for study and replacing them after use, were cumbersome. The new accommodation houses the archives in a properly controlled environment. The search room is adjacent. And the collections of both books and archives are a great deal more accessible to visitors through the provision of exhibition facilities both here and on the tourist route within the chapel itself.

The undercroft, which is situated below the stone-built 15th-century dining hall of the priest vicars, lies at the foot of a slope but is not fully below ground. A suite of rooms at this level, some of which once formed the organist's house, has been very successfully converted into two archive strongrooms and a search room, linked by a corridor fitted with exhibition display cases.

Behind a single outer fire door are two archive strongrooms. The walls of this sturdy building were thick enough not to require significant alteration during the conversion, but (after archaeological investigation) new load-bearing concrete floors were laid to support mobile racking. Above the ceilings a waterproof membrane was inserted to protect the archives from any ingress of water from above, and as an added precaution new drains were laid below the floor. The ceilings were

made fireproof, to give all-round 4hr fire protection, and an FM200® fire-suppression system was also fitted. The rooms are fully air-conditioned and mechanically ventilated to achieve stability within BS 5454.

In the same development, but towards the rear of the building, two new stack rooms for the library's special book collection were constructed, one above the other. An ingenious air handling system ensures that air circulates behind and through the book shelves and through connecting vents in the floor/ceiling separating the two rooms so that for purposes of environmental control the two spaces are treated as one. These rooms are handsomely fitted out with sealed wooden shelving and are spacious enough to allow small groups of visitors to be shown the books.

The comfortably-appointed search room has space for up to 5 readers, whilst a smaller room adjacent is provided with computer terminals for access to the catalogue. The accommodation is completed, on the upper floors of the building, by staff offices, a kitchen and WC.

This is a cost-effective and strikingly successful conversion of an historic building.

Architects: In-house (Surveyor of the Fabric). Cost: around £310,000, of which £234,000 was provided by the HLF and the remainder by benefactors.

Shropshire Records and Research Centre

Shrewsbury

Purpose-built, 1995

This development comprises two linked buildings on a town centre site. It is situated on steeply sloping ground near the railway station, and nestles below what is now the county library headquarters (but was once the historic grammar school, dating from the 16th century).

A three-storey library building which was already on the site was adapted to provide staff offices for the archive service on the top floor and an archive strongroom in the basement. The library retains the ground floor in between.

Alongside this, and linked to it, is a fine purpose-built building of three storeys, attractively faced in red brick. At the front, this is set back from the main road down a short lane. The site is pleasantly landscaped and the approach path has a representation of the county arms in coloured pebbles with the motto *Floreat Salopia*. Roads at lower levels allow a good general view of the building from the rear, and provide access for archive deliveries.

Because of the lie of the land, the public entrance, reception area, and search room are on the uppermost of the new building's three levels. The floor below houses, among other functions, the conservation workshop and one of the repositories, whilst the lowest level, recessed into the hillside but with road access to the rear, houses a third archive repository.

The site, and thus the scope for the allocation of functions, was tightly constrained, but it was owned by the county council, was all that was available, and was very central, so it was perhaps worth accepting some resulting inconveniences. The levels of the two buildings do not line up, so stairs were necessary wherever there is a link. There was no space for a dedicated loading bay with adjacent document reception room, so documents arriving enter, in effect, directly into the basement repository. A room above, adjacent to the conservation workshop, was originally fitted out as a reception and cleaning room, but has since been adapted for reprographic services. Non-archival storage space is in very short supply, and there is no meeting or seminar room.

The building was designed with heavy mass and insulation (the repository's inside walls being of concrete block), in order to avoid the need for air-conditioning. The repositories are windowless, and there is no air change/ventilation other than that provided by the opening and closing of doors during the working day. Built-in electric fans are available in each repository to assist air circulation if needed. Dehumidifiers are used when necessary, and there is a hot water heating pipe (fitted with leak detectors) but this is hardly ever used. With this strategy of minimal intervention, environmental conditions remain broadly stable within BS 5454 recommendations, although there is slight solar gain in summer in one repository. An automatic water-sprinkler fire-suppression system is provided in just one of the repositories.

The public search room, which has been adapted several times to meet changing demands, has designated areas for consulting books and finding aids, microforms and online resources. An etched glass screen, with words commissioned from a local poet, seperates off a quieter working space for readers wishing to consult original archival materials.

Cost: around £1.8 million, funded by the County Council.

Southampton University Library Special Collections

Purpose-built extension, 2004

In the course of a wider development of the University Library between 2002 and 2004, the space previously allocated to Special Collections was significantly redeveloped and expanded on two sides into a completely new library extension. The building was at the design stage as BS 5454:2000 was being published, so the project was able to take the new standard fully into account. For once the claim in the commemorative booklet for the official opening that the accommodation 'rivals the best facilities nationally' is no exaggeration.

The new space includes an additional strongroom, highly specified for security and fire resistance and fitted with mobile racking which will provide expansion space for an estimated 20 years. Here and in the two existing strongrooms (which could also be converted to mobile racking when required for further expansion) an Inergen® fire-suppression system linked to an aspirating detection and alarm system has replaced the halon previously in use. A mineral fire retardant has been sprayed on ceilings to improve their fire rating in this shared building.

The premises are air-conditioned through-out, with a new computer-monitored air-handling system designed to deliver different ambient conditions and different levels of filtration for the building's various functions. These include for the first time a separate store equipped with freezers for volatile and sensitive materials, such as nitrate film,. The fine suite of conservation studios has separate wet, dry and chemical zones. Other technical facilities include a reprographics studio and dark room. As an example of the careful attention to detail often overlooked elsewhere, even the corridors are tanked and equipped with drains to allow for effective cleaning and the dispersal of water in any emergency.

Public facilities include a new, larger search room for up to 20 readers and a seminar room for up to 12 readers, invigilated in the same secure area so that original documents can be produced in the course of teaching or research. A new exhibition gallery at the entrance to the department allows access to other users of the library and to the general public for what will become a regular series of short-term exhibitions. The exhibition cases are lit by fibre optic lighting and are individually climatised.

Consultant architects: Wilson Mason and Partners.
Cost: approximately £3 million (within a total cost of around £10 million for the library development as a whole), funded by the university, supported by significant grants from the HLF (around £800,000), the Jewish Claims Conference (US $75,000), and private benefactors.
New storage: strongroom, 196.5 sq.m.; quarantine area 22.1 sq.m.; volatile store 20.8. sq.m.
Published references: *The Hartley Library, University of Southampton 2004* (booklet for the official opening) and website references. Search room photo courtesy of Southampton University.

Surrey History Centre

Goldsworth Road, Woking

Purpose-built, 1998 (See Appendix for Plan)

Surrey History Centre was the first purpose-built archive building to receive a major grant (£2.74 million) from the HLF. Including the value of the site, the County Council contributed well over £4 million. The building, which brought together the functions and holdings of the former Surrey Record Office, the Guildford Muniment Room, the County Local Studies Library, the county Archaeology Unit and the museums development officer, was skilfully designed in such a way that a smaller building along similar lines could have been constructed had the application to HLF been unsuccessful.

In this simple and highly functionally-effective plan, there are three distinct but interlinked buildings, one behind the other. The public entrance, from Goldsworth Road, on the north side under a rather startling heavy canopy, leads into the first building, which contains all the public facilities (reception, search room, lecture/seminar and exhibition space). This in turn shields the whole of one long wall of the repository block in the second building from contact with the external environment. The space designed for the county archaeology unit performs a similar function along one of the short walls of the repository. The third building, housing staff offices, conservation and technical services, protects the other long wall of the repository at the rear. So in all, only one end wall of the repository is exposed to external climatic conditions.

The repository is constructed on a concrete and steel frame faced with brick. Despite its energy-efficient design, full air-conditioning has been provided. This has proved a mixed blessing, as repeated hiccups in different parts of the system have made the maintenance of a stable environment more challenging than had been hoped. The repository is on a single floor, rising through two storeys, racked to a height of 4 metres and therefore requiring high, portable step-ladders for staff access. An automatic Argonite® fire-suppression system is fitted, with independent controls for each of the three repositories. Internal steel roller blinds at each door provide additional fire protection.

The design as a whole has proved amenable to adaptation in the light of the changing needs of the Centre. For example, the lecture room and exhibition space has been fitted with sliding partitions to allow for a variety of public and educational uses, and a digitisation studio has replaced the original photographic studio. There are plans to develop the large entrance foyer to provide additional public amenities. The latter area already makes a strong statement about Surrey's historic past, with a colourful and interesting Surrey tapestry designed by Philip Sanderson and woven at the West Dean Tapestry Studio, and two large panels, 'Surrey in glass', engraved by Martin Donlin, both these works of art having been funded by the Arts Lottery Fund.

Architects: W S Atkins.
Cost: around £7 million.
Storage: 1,487 sq.m.
Published references: D Robinson, 'Surrey History Centre, the experience of lottery application,' in *JSA* 18, no 2 (1997), pp.151-63. Surrey History Centre website: www.surreycc. gov.uk/surreyhistoryservice

Tameside Local Studies and Archives Centre
Ashton under Lyne

Purpose-built, 2005

On the former car park of Ashton Central Library, a self-contained two-storey building faced in stone to about a height of 4 ft and red brick for the remainder, and with a slate-covered pitched roof, has been constructed to house the new Local Studies and Archives Centre. The previous premises in Stalybridge were cramped and unsatisfactory. Here, by contrast, there is a sense of spaciousness – at least for the public reading room and the storage areas, although the staff accommodation is windowless and by no means generous in size.

The building is linked by a glass atrium to the Central Library, which provides the main access route for the public. Having such an important kindred facility adjacent is doubly appealing, as it not only facilitates collaboration among the staff of the two services but also enables some of the cleaning and maintenance costs to be shared.

The large reading room, on the ground floor, has good sight-lines and its generous floor and wall space has not only enabled the shelving of the most popular books from the local studies collection on open access, but also the designation of distinct spaces for users of PCs (6), microfiche (4), microfilm (8) and books and archives (8).

Apart from the staff offices, the remainder of the ground floor and the whole of the first floor are secure storage areas, air-conditioned to BS 5454 standard and protected by fire doors, an aspiration fire detection and alarm system and intruder alarms. The internal walls are of concrete blockwork, and where these also run along the external walls they are separated from the external brick cladding by an insulated cavity wall. Most of the plant is housed in the open air outside, partly sheltered by the generous overhang of the roof. The internal space below the pitched roof is fitted with louvred vents which provide the air intake and ventilate the roof space.

Architects: Cruikshank & Seward.
Cost: £1 million, plus £60,000 fitting out. Met entirely by the Council.

Tate Gallery Library and Archive
Hyman Kreitman Research Centre
Tate Britain, London

Converted gallery picture store, 2002

After many years of unsuccessful searching for archive storage worthy of this pre-eminent national collection, the Tate Gallery Archive finally moved into a purpose-converted unit, on-site within Tate Britain, Millbank, in 2002. The conversion and fitting out of the new Centre were made possible by a generous donation of £2.2 million by a single benefactor, Hyman Kreitman. The long wait has been amply rewarded and the results are a credit both to the gallery and the Kreitman Foundation.

A former picture storage area, on the Tate's lower ground floor, was the site eventually chosen. It was a location that presented a number of risks and challenges. As Tate Britain is close to the Thames and this area

is below flood level, the storage space has been tanked and equipped with strong flood-barrier doors. The absence of windows and the presence of low ceilings might have made for a forbidding working environment, but this has been well compensated for by the use of coffered ceilings to give an impression of greater overall height, the quality and style of lighting, and the use of glass panels to mimic windows at intervals round the walls of the reading rooms. The constraints of space meant that staff offices had to be located elsewhere in the Gallery.

Two separate research rooms are provided: respectively for the Library and the Archives. The former seats about 28 and the latter about 16 readers, at specially designed tables with

recessed power supplies for laptops. Whilst columns are a significant feature of the Library reading room, the Archive search room is clear of these and has excellent sight-lines for invigilation.

Library and Archive storage are physically separated from each other by a mesh screen with a security card system that limits access into the Archive stores to departmental staff only, while allowing Tate staff users into the Library stores. Otherwise all the collections (books, art work, paper and audio-visual archives) share the same storage environment, in a large rectangular space to the rear of the research area, which is divided into three compartments for effective fire control. It has proved difficult to achieve the right degree of stability for relative humidity from an air-conditioning system that does not serve the Research Centre exclusively but a whole quadrant of the Gallery. Fire protection strategy is based on an aspirating detection and alarm system and the gallery's 24-hour security presence.

Architects: John Miller & Partners.
Cost: £2.2 million.
Storage: *c.* 4.2km of archive shelving plus 14.4 cu.m. plan chest storage.
Published references: B Houghton, 'The Hyman Kreitman Research Centre for the Tate Library and Archive', in *Art Libraries Journal* no 27/4 (2004) p.19ff.

The National Archives

Kew

Public Record Office second building
(since 2003 The National Archives)
Purpose-built, 1995 (See Appendix for plan)

The first PRO building on this site was featured as a case study in *ABUK 1*. The second, which was on the drawing board in the late 1980s and completed in 1995, is of a markedly different design, altogether more human and less austere on first approach. As the site was being developed the opportunity was also taken to rethink the landscaping as an integral part of the overall design, for example combining the functionality of balancing ponds (to control rainwater run-off and potential flooding) with the ambience of a pleasant water-garden as an additional local amenity. At the planning stage there was extensive discussion with the neighbouring communities to ensure that the project secured strong local support. High quality materials were specified, both inside and out, as befitting a building of such outstanding importance to the nation's heritage. Other planning objectives for the building itself, including energy efficiency and easy and cost-effective maintenance, have on the whole been met, although some features

are reported to be awkwardly inaccessible for cleaning and maintenance. As far as equipment and services are concerned, improvement to energy efficiency is an ongoing target in the light of ISO 14001 accreditation.

The archive storage accommodation, built with a reinforced concrete frame on raft foundations, comprises four floors, each with three separate repositories containing mostly mobile racking. The building's structure is of heavy mass, well insulated, and has been found capable of maintaining environmental conditions without mechanical assistance for up to three days. But in order to maintain stable environmental conditions within BS 5454 recommendations air-conditioning is provided. Conditions are monitored by a computerised BMS, and can be separately controlled in each repository as required. Positive air pressure is maintained within the storage areas to minimise changes to storage conditions with the opening of doors and the coming and going of staff. The external wall area of the

repository is minimised by siting circulating space, technical services and staff offices predominantly to the south and west. This provides both an environmental buffer against direct sunlight affecting the walls of storage areas and a visual softening of the overall appearance of the building.

An automatic fire-suppression system was discussed, but in the end not implemented. Instead, fire control strategy relies first on the division of the repository into separate compartments, and secondly on early detection and alarm and quick response.

In addition to the repositories, the building also includes two-storey accommodation with, to the rear, an executive suite and conference, training and interview facilities; and to the front, a conservation workshop, an education suite and staff offices. The latter are separated from the repository by a generously wide, tree-lined internal avenue under a glass roof, which provides plenty of natural light for the adjacent offices. Externally, the offices are protected from solar glare by overhanging canopies on a lightweight frame.

The specific needs of a building of the impressive size and scale of The National Archives called for a number of solutions that are unique among UK archive buildings and might not be necessary in buildings of a smaller scale. Documents are delivered from the repositories in 'Kew II' to the reading rooms in 'Kew I' by means of an automated (TeleLift) system of containers suspended from a monorail. Dedicated engineering staff are on hand to maintain this vital internal transit system. The glazed roof of the atrium is fitted with automatic sun-blinds. Some of the roof-light windows are also set to open automatically in the event of a fire, to let out smoke and combustible gases and prevent flash-over.

Architects: Property Services Agency.
Cost: over £30 million.
Storage capacity: 15,500 sq. metres.
Published references: Public Record Office extension: preliminary sketch plan report. Stage 3 (PSA Projects, October 1989), available in TNA Library.

Unilever Archives

Port Sunlight

Converted premises and offices within factory precinct, 2004

Unilever archives, together with some of the company's other administrative functions, now occupy a free-standing red-brick building on the Port Sunlight factory site. The library/search room, which can seat 8 readers in comfort but is flexible enough to be used for other meetings and group visits, is on the first floor, entered via a large and comfortably-appointed open-plan staff office. Staff can also consult sound and film archives in an adjacent audio-visual room.

The archive storage, at lower ground floor level, ie two floors below, occupies a converted suite of rooms which already had concrete floors with good floor-loading capacity from their previous duties as a plant room and a development centre for testing detergents. Most of the building's existing internal wall structures and the internal fire doors were retained in situ, to make a total of 8 store rooms, a document reception room and a boxing room. To enhance fire resistance and environmental control, ventilation grilles in the existing fire doors were blocked up, and any gaps in dividing walls and ceilings were fire-stopped. The rooms were re-painted and provided with new fire alarms, and in order to meet the recommendations of BS 5454 each room was equipped with one or more air-conditioning units (apart, that is, from two small rooms with a grille in the party wall, which share one unit). This allows different environmental parameters to be set for different media, a useful facility for a large business archive holding not only archives in various media (paper, photographs, artwork, sound, video and film), but also many artefacts associated with the history of the constituent companies. To round off the risk management, the rooms were fitted with a new fire detection and alarm system, and the drains below floor level (and also the floor above) were fitted with water alarms.

This cost-effective conversion of a basically robust building has provided much improved facilities for both archives and staff.

Architects: KKA Architects.
Cost: c.£698,000.
Storage: 3.7 km.
Published reference: 'The opening of Unilever Archives', in *ARC* 189 (May 2005), p.13.

University of Warwick Modern Records Centre and BP Archives
Coventry

Purpose-built as part of the University Library extension, 1993

This building, which was opened just too late for inclusion in *ABUK 1* and is therefore one of the oldest to be featured in the present volume, is showing remarkably few signs of ageing, and from the archival point of view continues to perform very well. So does the imaginative partnership – still unique in the UK – between business and university. Each partner has separate storage and office accommodation but there is a common suite of public rooms and a common area for document reception and sorting. The archive facilities occupy the ground floor and semi-basement, with two floors of university library accommodation

above, linked to the main library by a glazed bridge. All floors of the building have been specified with the same floor-loading, and the columns rise through the building's full height.

A light and spacious entrance lobby, with WCs and coat and bag deposit off, leads into the main search room, where readers each have generously large individual tables on which to spread out papers and research materials. On BP's side of the search room a glass partition leads into a room originally planned for the consultation of confidential material. In practice no separate room has been required for this purpose, and instead it has been equipped with video facilities and is used for seminars and other potentially noisy activities. Attractive exhibition screens are mounted on its walls. The roles of this and the main search room can be reversed when there is a need for larger meetings.

The archive storage accommodation has been designed with all-round 4-h fire resistance. Both units also have aspirating detection and alarm systems. In addition, BP's storage, but not that of the Modern Records Centre, is equipped with a dry-pipe water sprinkler system for fire fighting. All the storage is air-conditioned, and on the whole the system performs well, providing a stable environment within BS 5454. A cooler room originally intended for the storage of photographs has now been reserved for film storage; as the photographs are consulted regularly they are stored in the main strongroom in order to avoid the need for acclimatisation before use.

Architects: WF Johnson and partners.
Cost: about £2 million, of which BP provided £1.5 m.
Storage: Modern Records Centre 11.863 km.

Warwickshire Record Office

Priory Park, Warwick

Conversion and purpose-built extension, 2003

Uniquely among the buildings in this book, Warwickshire Record Office in effect re-invented itself without moving from its existing site, by extending the earlier record office building in three different directions and radically rethinking the previous layout, reversing the siting of public and staff functions. The purpose-built extensions provide additional storage accommodation (on two floors), a new public entrance and reception area, and an addition to what has become, under the new arrangements, the public search room.

Priory Park, the grounds of a historic house (which has long since disappeared apart from one long red-brick wall and a range of buildings originating in the 17th century), was a sensitive and difficult site to develop further. Archaeological excavations were required before building work on the extensions could proceed, and the edge of the hillside and woodland on which it is built rigidly determined the maximum footprint of the new storage block, which is very close to overhanging trees.

The two new strongrooms are of brick with insulated cavity walls. The upper floor is topped by a concrete slab, above which is a pitched roof with concrete tiles. The block has been built on to the original outside wall of the first strongroom block, and the two rooms are entered through new fire doors breached in that wall at each level. The rooms are fully air-conditioned and fitted with an aspirating detection and alarm system and an Inergen® fire-suppression system. They are planned to provide accrual space for up to 25 years.

The lie of the land meant that there had to be a flight of steps up to the reception desk in the new public entrance, and a lift has therefore been provided to assist access by the disabled. The reception area doubles as a sales point, and there is a comfortable refreshment room for readers, with a self-service drinks machine (and behind the scenes a similar room for staff). WCs and an Events Room for meetings are immediately adjacent.

The third extension has created the space for a much enlarged and re-located search room

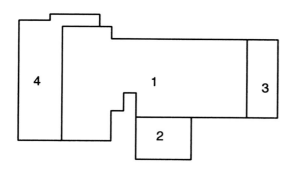

*(1) main building prior to current work 2-4
    extensions:*
(2) reception,
(3) search room,
(4) storage

with separate zones for consultation of original archives, microfilm, microfiche and online and other catalogue resources.

The one remaining range of 17th-century buildings, free-standing at right-angles to the main building, comes complete with panelled walls and in one room a fine plastered ceiling, and was therefore the most sensitive to adapt. It has been well fitted out as a conservation and digitisation suite comprising a number of separate and rather small rooms for functions where ideally plenty of space is required for both equipment and circulation. Within these constraints good use has been made of the available space.

The overall result of the new arrangements is a remarkable transformation of a cramped and difficult building into a bright and up-to-date facility which is altogether better appointed in terms of logistics, and provides essential public amenities that were simply not possible in the earlier building.

Architects: Corstorphine & Wright.
Cost: £2.3 million, of which £1.3 m was provided by the HLF and the remainder by the county council with a contribution from the Friends of the Record Office.
Storage: (linear capacity of the new strongrooms) 3.2 km.

York University: Borthwick Institute for Archives
Heslington, York

Purpose-built, 2005

The Borthwick Institute previously occupied a medieval guildhall in the city centre which, although steeped in history, could never meet today's best standards for storage and public access. With an extension planned to the Raymond Burton library on the University's campus at Heslington, the opportunity came to make a concurrent bid to the HLF to extend that project further to include a new, purpose-built Borthwick Institute, adjoining the library but with its own distinctive character.

The building is impressively located on top of an earth bank. Its public face is anything but four-square, combining graceful curves and sharp angularity to add visual interest. It is faced in two different shades of terracotta tiles and, unusually among recent archive buildings, the sloping metal roof has no overhang beyond the walls but is contained within the parapet and drained internally through concealed service shafts so that there are no external rainwater goods and from most angles the roof itself is invisible. The building's orientation is beneficial, with most of the staff work rooms and the conservation workshop facing north or north west. Baffles have been added to the exterior of the search room to deflect sunlight.

Public facilities are mostly on the first floor, with a generous reception and reference room leading (via a glazed door controlled from reception) into the principal search room which can comfortably seat 20 readers. The search room tables, crafted by Treske in solid ash, were designed in-house and include recessed bookshelves to house documents awaiting consultation. A separate large table is provided for maps. All seating is fully adjustable. Wireless computer connections are available throughout. Adjacent to the main reading room is a windowless, self-service microfilm reading room which can be accessed direct from the landing at hours when the Library is open to readers but the Institute closed. On the second

floor is an exhibition hall, adjacent to two
seminar or meeting rooms which can be opened
up into one.

Technical services include a fully equipped
conservation studio with a tanked area for
wet processes, and a metal-lined cold store for
special media.

Archive storage is on two levels (ground
and first floors), and includes the most
extensive electronic mobile shelving in any
new UK archive repository. The building's
heavy mass and insulation play the major part
in maintaining the stability of the storage
environment, making as much use as possible
of passive control, although after extensive
computer modelling a mechanical air-handling
system was also supplied, controlled by a
computerised BMS. An aspirating detection
and alarm system is linked 24 hours to on-site
security.

Staff offices and workrooms have been nicely
appointed, many of them off a central room
lined with books, and with comfortable seating
in the middle, having something of a senior
common room ambience. Further details are
given in the published references cited below.

Architects: Leach Rhodes Walker.
Engineers: Buro Happold.
Storage: 1500 cu.m.
Cost: approximately £6.5 million within a
larger project of £9 m, including a grant of
£4.4 m from HLF and a benefaction of £2 m
from Raymond Burton, the balance contributed
by the University and other benefactors.
Published references: 'New for old. A modern
facility for Europe's finest archive collection',
in *Building Services Journal*, December 2004,
pp.26-30. On the shelving see advertising
feature in *ARC 196* (Dec 2005).

APPENDIX

Jersey Archive
St Helier, Jersey, Channel Islands

Purpose-built, 2000

Jersey Archive was a pioneer in the use of natural climatisation without recourse to air-conditioning. As the process, and the scientific thinking behind it, has been described in some detail, with illustrations, in the published references cited at the end of this case study, only a short summary is attempted here.

The building sits in the bowl of what was once a stone quarry. This offers protection against strong winds and other extremes of weather, and the rock face has been stabilised and netted to prevent slippage. The perimeter of the property is therefore clearly defined, and at the only entrance to the bowl a handsome *porte-cochère* with a metal gate provide added security without significantly obstructing the view of the impressive building within, which makes a fine statement about Jersey's archival heritage.

There are in essence four linked blocks, each with their own distinctive architectural

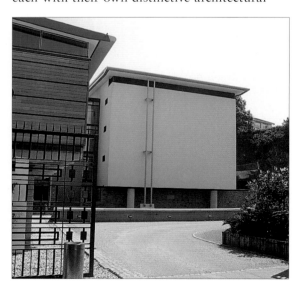

features. Three of these, extending in a line away from the front gate, are of two storeys each, to house (a) reception, (b) public services and (c) staff offices, conservation and archive processing services. The axis then turns at right-angles for a link leading to the four-storey repository block. This zoning facilitates control of both security and the internal environment.

The public areas are bright, welcoming and innovative, with reception and meeting rooms downstairs and catalogue and search rooms upstairs. The spacious entrance foyer is large enough to hold receptions. It is extensively glazed, with panels of engraved glass and other commissioned artwork. The search room block is designed to look from the outside like a treasure chest with the lid raised, and is constructed in oak with the first floor jetted out beyond the ground floor. Inside, there is plentiful natural light.

The repository block, windowless, is of heavy mass (concrete blockwork), insulation and air-tightness (1 air change per day), and offers 4-h fire protection which is backed up by an Inergen® fire-suppression system. The wall cavity and roof space are ventilated. The walls on all sides are painted white, both outside and in, to reduce solar gain and heat loss. External air is monitored by a BMS to determine the (infrequent) occasions when conditions are favourable enough to allow fresh air intake. A fan-propelled down-draught or 'air curtain', generated from machinery fitted internally above the door in each strongroom, is activated automatically when the door is opened, to prevent air migrating in either direction across the threshold and destabilising the storage environment. A small amount of heating (from warm water carried between the inner and outer skins of the building) and dehumidification are available when required, but there is no air-conditioning system. The ability of the building fabric itself to breathe, absorbing and giving out moisture at different times, has been harnessed towards the control of RH. Despite the undeniable energy-efficiency of the building, it has not proved plain sailing to maintain temperature and RH absolutely within the parameters recommended by BS 5454 all year round. In part this is because, inevitably, large parts of the storage space were at first unoccupied, with the result that the environment performed rather differently there than in the occupied space, and in part because the upper floors in particular tended to experience extended peaks of temperature in summer. The only parts to be mechanically climatised are the two cooler storage rooms on the ground floor for special media.

Architects: MacCormac Jamieson Prichard. BDK Design Associates.
Engineers: Ove Arup & Partners.
Storage: 3.12 km.
Published references: A Pearson, 'Totally absorbing [Jersey Archive, St Helier], in *Building*, 6 August 1999 pp. 44-5. B Lloyd, 'New purpose-built Jersey Archive opens', in Society of Archivists *Newsletter* 134 (Aug/Sept 2000) pp.9-10. D Williams, 'Defining an archive: the Jersey experience', in *JSA* 22 no.1 (2001) pp.125-38. S Kennett, 'Soaking up the atmosphere', in *Building Services Journal*, August 2001 pp.51-2.

Simplified plans of selected UK archive buildings

The following plans (all in the horizontal plane) show the general relationship between functions. Although based on true plans they are not exactly to scale, nor are the sketches each drawn to the same scale. For security reasons a number of details such as doors have been omitted. Areas shaded grey represent archive storage, hatched areas stairs or lift unless otherwise indicated.

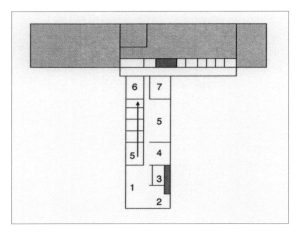

Berkshire: First floor (public services are below)

1 conservation (dry)	5 staff offices
2 conservation (wet)	6 library/conference
3 microfilming	7 staff room.
4 administration	

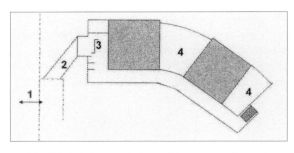

English Heritage, National Monuments Record

1 original GWR building	3 acclimatisation area
2 link	4 plant

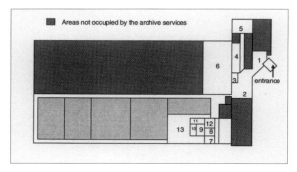

Devon: Ground floor

1 reception	8 cleaning
2 refreshments	9 sorting
3 lockers	10 chemicals
4 WCs	11 dark room
5 lecture	12 cataloguing
6 search	13 conservation
7 document reception	

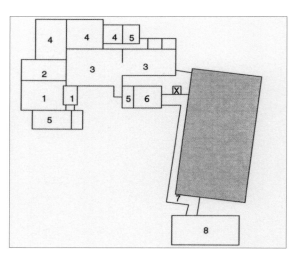

Leicestershire, Leicester and Rutland: Ground floor

1 public entrance and reception	5 WCs
2 education/meeting	6 reprographics
3 search	7 enclosed walkway
4 staff	8 storage (with conservation above)

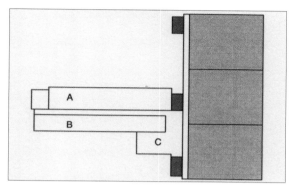

National Archives of Scotland, Thomas Thomson
House: General (horizontal) profile (3 floors)
A (ground) sorting; (1st) conservation; (2nd)
   offices
B (ground) temp. storage; (1st) offices; (2nd) open
   area
C (ground) loading bay; (1st) plant; (2nd) plant

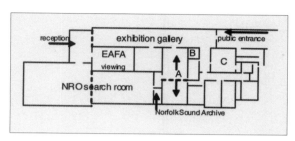

Norfolk: public areas in more detail
A Green room
B attendant
C common room

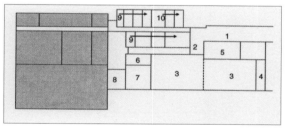

Norfolk: Ground floor (part)

1 exhibition
2 reception
3 NRO search
4 sound archive
   search
5 EAFA viewing

6 issue
7 NRO general office
8 county archivist
9 EAFA processing
   rooms
10 EAFA staff rooms

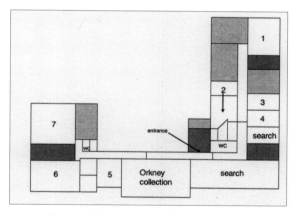

Orkney Library and Archive: First floor

1 document reception
2 photo archive suite
3 biodiversity room
4 staff

5 family history
6 exhibition/meeting
7 education

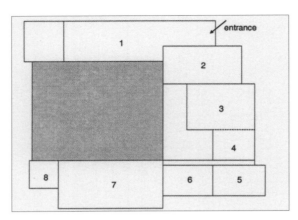

Oxfordshire: Ground floor

1 public reception   *5 staff*
2 exhibition   *6 education*
3 search   *7 conservation*
4 microfilm   *8 loading bay*

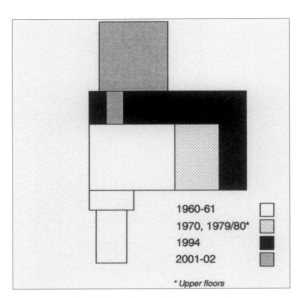

Staffordshire: Ground floor extensions

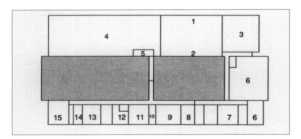

Surrey: Ground floor

1 main entrance   *10 drying*
2 reception   *11 assistants'*
3 events/meetings   *workroom*
4 search   *12 cleaning/freezing*
5 document   *13 plant*
production   *14 reprographics*
6 archaeology unit   *15 packaging*
7 staff common room   *(additional staff*
8 education   *workrooms and*
9 document reception   *conservation on 1st*
and sorting   *floor)*

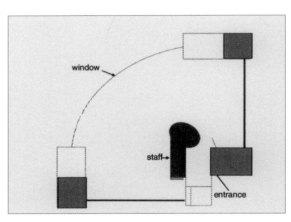

City of Westminster Archives Centre: Reading room (5th floor)

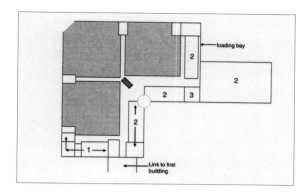

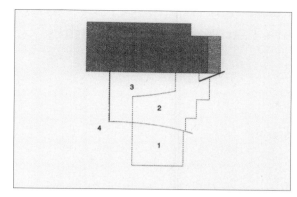

The National Archives, Kew, second building:
Ground floor
1 conference and training
2 offices
3 education

York University, Borthwick Institute for Archives:
First floor
1 public reception
2 search
3 microfilm
4 entrance lobby/
  links to other parts
  of the library

Published References for UK Archive Buildings not featured as Case Studies

Ayrshire
Wilbraham, K, 'Ayrshire Archives', in *Scottish Archives* 6 (2000), pp.83-93.

Birmingham (RC) Archdiocesan Archives
Sharp, J, 'Birmingham archdiocesan archives', in *Catholic Archives* 22 (2002), pp.6-9.

Croydon Central Library
Harrison, D, *Library buildings in the United Kingdom 1990-1994* (1995), pp.110-11.

Lancaster University: Ruskin Library
See CABE case study at www.cabe.org.uk/library/

Leeds University Brotherton Library, West Building Extension
Harrison, D, *Library buildings in the United Kingdom 1990-1994* (1995), pp. 25-7.

Leonard Cheshire Archive
'Building a new repository for a charity archive' , in *ARC* 196 (Dec. 2005), pp.7-8.

National Library of Scotland
Kidd, S, *Fire risk management in historic buildings* (Historic Scotland, Technical Conservation Research and Education Division, Technical Advice Note 22 (2001). Includes a case study : 'The National Library of Scotland: risk improvement in a major national institution'.
Kitching, C, 'Preservation in new buildings', in *LIBER Quarterly*, 10 no 2 (2000), pp.376-86.

Suffolk Record Office, Lowestoft
Jenkins, G, 'Winning by design: Lowestoft Library and Records Office', in *Public Library Journal*, Spring 2004, pp.10-12. Also featured in the database of www.designinglibraries.org.uk

University of London Institute of Education
Harrison, D, *Library buildings in the United Kingdom 1990-1994* (1995), pp.31-3.

Archive Building Projects in the UK completed 1993-2005 [Total 108]

* indicates that the building is covered in one of the case studies in this volume

NEW PURPOSE-BUILDS AND EXTENSIONS [Total 42]

National [5]: British Library*, Jersey*, National Archives of Scotland (Thomas Thomson House)*, National Library of Wales (Third building)*, TNA* (Kew II).

Higher Education [16]: Cambridge: Churchill*, Girton*, Lucy Cavendish, Newnham, University Library; East Anglia Film Archive* (UEA [see Norfolk]), Glasgow (Special Collections)*, Lancaster (Ruskin Library), Leeds (Brotherton Library), Northern Region Film and TV Archive (Teesside)*, Nottingham (exhibition centre), Open University Library, Oxford: St Hilda's, Warwick (Modern Records Centre and BP Archives)*, York (Borthwick Institute)*.

Local authority record offices/archive services [14]: Berkshire, Croydon, Dumfries, Essex*, London Metropolitan Archives*, Newham, Norfolk*, Orkney*, Perth & Kinross*, Shropshire*, Staffordshire, Surrey*, Tameside*, Westminster.

Business [1] BP* [see above, University of Warwick].

Other specialist repositories: [6] Cardinal Tomás Ó Fiaich Memorial Library and Archive*, Hereford Cathedral Library*, Leonard Cheshire Archive, Wordsworth Museum (Jerwood Centre), York Minster Library, Yorkshire Film Archive*.

PART NEW, PART CONVERSION [Total 9]

National [1]: English Heritage National Monuments Record*.

Higher Education [2]: Oxford: All Souls College, Southampton*.

Local authority record offices/archive services [4]: Gloucestershire*, Kent (East Kent), Leicestershire*, Warwickshire*.

Business [1]: Diageo

Other specialist repositories [1]: Royal Geographical Society.

CONVERSION (premises converted to archival use for the first time) [Total 28]

National: [-].

Higher Education [4]: Cambridge: Gonville & Caius; North West Film Archive (Manchester Metropolitan), University College London (interim premises).

Local authority record offices/archive services [16]: Angus, Ayrshire, Bury (Manchester), Carmarthenshire, Cumbria (Whitehaven)*, Devon*, East Riding of Yorkshire (interim premises), Greenwich, Hertfordshire, North Highland (Wick), Oxfordshire*, Rochdale, Stirling, Wirral, Wolverhampton, Worcestershire Family History Centre.

Business [5]: BT, Barclays Group, Guardian/ Observer, News International, Unilever.

Other specialist repositories [3]: Birmingham RC archdiocese, Elgar Birthplace, St George's Chapel Windsor*.

IN SITU CONVERSION/ REFURBISHMENT [Total 29]

National [3]: Parliamentary Archive (House of Lords), National Library of Scotland (George IV Bridge), Tate Gallery*.

Higher Education [8]: British Library of Political and Economic Science (LSE), Durham, Edinburgh, London: Institute of Education, School of Oriental and African Studies, University Library (Senate House); Oxford: Oriel; Sheffield.

Local authority record offices/archive services [8]: Bristol, Denbighshire*, Dorset, Manchester City, Oswestry, Peterborough, Stoke-on-Trent, Suffolk (Lowestoft).

Business [3]: Bank of England, Cable & Wireless, Rothschild.

Other specialist repositories [7]: Brentwood RC diocese, Charterhouse School, Church of England Record Centre, Dartington Hall, Linen Hall Library (Belfast), Royal Academy of Arts, Royal Society of Arts.

NOTES

Abbreviations

ABUK1	Kitching, *Archive buildings in the United Kingdom 1977-1992*
BMS	Building Management System
BS 5454	*British Standard 5454:2000, Recommendations for the storage and exhibition of archival documents*
BSI *Guide*	*Archival Documents. Guide to the interpretation of BS5454:2000* (British Standards Institution PD 0024:2001)

HE	Higher education
JSA	*Journal of the Society of Archivists*
MLA	The Museums, Libraries and Archives Council
RH	relative humidity
TNA	The National Archives
u/v	ultra-violet

Works cited in the footnotes simply by author are more fully referenced in the Bibliography.

Introduction

1. The actual total is impossible to calculate because many archive developments fall within larger projects for university and national libraries where the archive component has not been separately costed. Projects for which the cost is known readily add up to £150m, and the scale and number of the rest makes the figure of £250m not unreasonable.
2. For a general introduction to archives in the UK see Kitching, *Archives. The very essence of our heritage* (1996).
3. Kitching (2000) and (2001).
4. www.nationalarchives.gov.uk/archives/framework/ and links from that page.
5. www.ncaonline.org.uk/
6. See its report, *Listening to the past, speaking to the future* (2004).
7. www.a2a.org.uk/
8. Such as Very Early Smoke Detection Apparatus (VESDA®). See chapter 7.
9. Although Jersey is not in the United Kingdom it is embraced within the Society of Archivists and is therefore included, by agreement, in this study.
10. Museums Association, *Guidelines on pollution control in museum buildings* (2000).
11. Padfield (1999).
12. www.ica.org then link to 'download center'.
13. See Bibliography.
14. For libraries, see for example www.designinglibraries.org.uk, and the monumental work of Leighton and Weber. For museums, see, among others Bordass and Cassar.

Chapter 1: Archives and Archive buildings

1. Setting on one side the generally small amounts of space that may be gained from the de-accessioning of unused (eg previously unappraised) materials.
2. On the definition and scope of archives see, for example Kitching (1996).
3. See, for example, Bell pp.85-89; Ratcliffe; Konya pp.20-23.

4. More formal stages of work, as far as the architects and engineers are concerned, are laid down in the RIBA Plan of Work and the ACE Work Stage respectively.
5. For more detailed guidance see in particular Leighton and Weber pp.8ff., Thompson p.27, and Salisbury esp. p.46ff.
6. 'Building a new repository for a charity archive', in *ARC* 196 (Dec. 2005), pp.7-8.
7. See BSI Guide pp.14-15. Other useful information may be found in the Chartered Institute of Building leaflet, *The procurement and management of construction* (www.ciob.org.uk) and other professional websites including those of CIBSE (www.cibse.org) and the Royal Institute of Chartered Surveyors (www.rics.org).
8. Only a few PFI schemes affecting archive buildings have been implemented to date, although others have been approved. The long-term costs including rent charges need careful consideration in the context of Whole Life Costing. There can be advantages, such as the contractor's obligation to maintain the building and services, with penalties for failure to do so.
9. Leighton and Weber p.331.
10. BSI *Guide* p.16.
11. C Twinn, 'Does research have a place in building projects?' in Cassar (ed) (1999), p.22.
12. See most recently, France (Direction des Archives de), *Les bâtiments d'archives 1986/2003* (2004).
13. Among works cited in the bibliography those by Bell, Bell & Faye, Buchmann, Duchein (1988), Faye, Gondos, Konya, and Leighton & Weber may be particularly commended. Their respective influences on the present volume are readily and gratefully acknowledged.
14. France (1970) p.572.
15. Buchmann, 'Planning an archive building' p.211.
16. Gondos pp.477-478.
17. This referral is mandatory in the case of certain controlled records including Public Records and Manorial and Tithe Documents.
18. The case for using the architect as project manager is defended by Salisbury p.109.

Chapter 2: Functions

1. This chapter seeks mainly to identify functions that are to be included in the plan for the building, and to draw attention to some of the problems that can arise. The space required for a number of functions, such as staff offices, might be laid down in the overall accommodation strategy of the parent authority. For comparative information on things that have gone wrong in other countries see Klasinc (2001) pp.126-128.

2. This is a widely reported phenomenon. At Tameside, for example, the reader figures went up by 33% in the first year after occupancy.

3. TNA and the National Archives of Scotland respectively offer this service.

4. Local practice as to the allocation of space between functions varies widely, and no attempt is made here to recommend standard or minimum dimensions. Useful guidance on individual rooms is given by Duchein (1988) and by Bell and Faye, but these and other authorities differ in detail.

5. See M Aleppo, 'Fumigation?'.

6. 'stacks' in library terminology.

7. This is recommended by Horsman p.76 (although it should not be of 'iron' as there stated).

8. For a detailed overview of racking issues see Ling p.71 ff.

9. See www.opsi.gov.uk/si/si2005/20050735.htm The Health and Safety Executive has published *The Work at Height Regulations 2005: A brief guide* (www.hse.gov.uk/pubns/indg401.pdf

10. Roper p.68; Woods (1992) p.132.

11. The guidance by Keene and Roper is still relevant but needs now to take more account of digitisation.

12. *The Pulman Guidelines*, 2nd edn 2003 (see www.pulmanweb.org) and the Disability Portfolio Guidelines (see www.mla.gov.uk under Libraries and Disability).

13. On the environment in display cases see especially Thomson (1986) and also the more detailed articles by him in *Studies in Conservation*, 9 and 22.

14. Very useful guidance on the layout of workstations and the circulating space required around each, is to be found in the American Library Association's *Building blocks for planning functional library space* (2001).

15. Thompson (1963) p.6.

16. This was still the predominant request at the Royal Historical Society's Gerald Aylmer seminar 2003 on the theme 'What do historians want from archives?'

17. For detailed guidance see Salisbury, esp. chapter 7.

18. Beware of rounding up sizes to the nearest 5 sq m, which can be a costly waste of space.

Chapter 3: The Site

Salisbury, p.13 discusses strategy for site selection.

1. J. Tiller, 'The new library building', in G Aylmer and J Tiller (eds), *Hereford cathedral. A history* (2000), p.313.

2. ex inf. John Hodgson, in a paper given to a Society of Archivists seminar held at the Borthwick Institute, York, 8 Feb. 2006 on 'Dealing with designers and builders'.

3. See case study, and Mead.

Chapter 4: Structure and Materials

1. Among recent works cited in the Bibliography, Giovannini's article gives a good summary of the issues.

2. Allsopp p.53.

3. BSI *Guide* ch.3.

4. Shields & Silcock p.167.

5. For France see Neirinck in *Atlanti* 2, p.53.

6. see chapter 6 below.

7. Matthews and Eden p.17.

8. See, for example, Crosby p.41

9. Pearson BP, 3.41-42.

10. Pearson BP, 4.20 cites an old adage that 'if you can't get into a building to fight the fire you lose the building!'

11. Elsewhere in Europe, a common specification for archives is to have a maximum of 200 square metres for any individual storage compartment. See for example, Giovannini p.9.

12. Duchein (1988) p.46.

13. See, for example, Centre for Sustainable Heritage report.

14. Lancaster University Library, Annual report 1996-1997.

15. BSI *Guide* p.12.

16. See, for example, *Drying Times* [newsletter of Harwell Drying and Restoration Services], 15 (summer 2001).

17. See, for example, Rowoldt.

18. A slow or nil indoor response to changes in the outdoor environmental conditions. For more detail see BSI *Guide* pp.16-17.

19. See Christoffersen. For earlier precedents, in Cologne, Koblenz and elsewhere in Europe, and in Suffolk and Northamptonshire in the UK, see *ABUK 1* pp.21-22.

20. For Jersey see Williams pp.130-131.

21. See for example Hanus p.29: a rise of 10°C accelerates chemical reactions by between 2 and 4 times.

22. This is despite the initial optimistic calculations described by Williams p.130.

23. Kitching (1993) p.19.

24. www.deepstore.co.uk/

25. As does Padfield (1997) and (1999).

26. Padfield (1999) p.8.

27. See particularly Cassar (1995 and 1995).

28. See article by Cox.

29. In the archival context see, for example, Klasinc (2002), p.23.

30. See, for example, Berge, DETR, Smith PF. See also the Building Research Establishment's Environmental Assessment Method (BREEAM), www.breeam.org/

31. 'Better buildings and open spaces can turn around the image of a neighbourhood', DCMS (2002) p.6.

32. See, for example, DETR (2000) p.34. Berge p.9 considers (though some might disagree) that 'twice as much damage to the environment can be tolerated for a building product that lasts 60 years compared with one that lasts 30 years'.

33. See Duchein (1988) pp.171-173.

34. This strategy, although sensible in itself, might

well impede longer-term expansion of the building.

35. *ABUK 1* p.21.
36. A point made by Ling, p.36ff, who also cites as another example the repository at Gatineau, Quebec.
37. Stonehouse and Stromberg p.49 suggest among the building's functions, 'to mark and honour the achievements of the human mind and spirit contained within its books and papers'.
38. Monumentality may be appropriate provided it does not sacrifice functionality. Ling p.15.
39. On this important point, as well as guidance on individual pollutants, see Museums Association, *Guidelines on pollution control*, p.15.
40. Thomson (1986) p.133.
41. Duchein in *Atlanti* 3 p.22.
42. Anderson in *Atlanti* 11 no 2.
43. In France, where Duchein extols the 'germicidal' properties of sunlight, it is nevertheless recommended that no more than 10% of repository wall should consist of windows: Duchein (1988) p.144.
44. Some 'ultra-violet' film is of doubtful quality. Specifications should be carefully checked before installation.
45. Collis p.53.

Chapter 5: Security

1. Among works cited in the Bibliography, attention is especially drawn to Leighton and Weber p.531, Dunn, and Feather & Eden.
2. Walch 1977/80, pp.1-2.
3. The use by the public of microform or digital surrogates of the most frequently consulted archives, rather than the originals, as the normal method of consultation also contributes to the security as well as the preservation of the originals.
4. Burke and Adeloye p.24.
5. Based at MLA.
6. Fire Protection Association, data sheet 14.
7. Burke and Adeloye pp.42-54; Simonet 1990.
8. Note that this has been revised subsequent to BS 5454:2000.
9. Neirinck in *Atlanti*, 3, p.34.

Chapter 6: Fire Prevention

1. BSI *Guide* ch. 3. For further reading see in particular the following works cited in the Bibliography: CIBSE (1997), International Council on Archives (ICA Studies, 11), Matthews and Eden, Neirinck in *Atlanti* 2 , BP Pearson and Woods (2002).
2. See BP Pearson (1995).
3. For accounts of fires in a number of other countries see *Atlanti* 2 (1993).
4. Shields and Silcock p.338.
5. See, for example, BP Pearson (1995) 3.27.
6. Neirinck, *Atlanti* 2 p.53; Matthews and Eden p.18, BP Pearson 3.29-30. P. Anderson in *Atlanti* 12 no 1.
7. For further information see www.vision-fs.com/
8. For an important evaluation of many existing options see Woods (2002). See also in particular CIBSE (1997).
9. See, for example, Shepilova.

10. See Australian Archives, *Guidelines* p.35. Also Ling p.58.
11. See Kitching (2000) and Kidd (2001).
12. Kitching (2000).
13. See the article by DP Smith.
14. P.Anderson, op.cit .
15. www.e1.greatlakes.com/wfp/common/jsp/index.jsp
16. Duchein (1988) p.101.
17. P. Anderson, op.cit. p.98.

Chapter 7: Environmental Control

1. Among works cited in the Bibliography, attention is particularly drawn to BS 5454 section 7, and to Thomson (1986).
2. For a fuller explanation see BSI *Guide* ch.4.
3. See, for example, Pinniger.
4. See, for example, BSI *Guide* p.32 and Cassar (ed) (1994) p.127.
5. See Bordass p.11.
6. Thomson (1965) p.157.
7. This is a requirement in some professional codes of practice.
8. On this topic see particularly Thomas; Thomson (1965); and Thomson (1988) pp. 130-58, 244-264.
9. The Meteorological Office publishes selected humidity statistics and a series of papers on the Climate of Great Britain, region by region.
10. Climate change and the historic environment.
11. There are a number of online sources for current information on air quality in the UK, such as www.airquality.co.uk/archive/index.php
12. Thomson (1965) p.152.
13. See particularly Museums Association, *Guidelines on pollution control*. Much useful information, arising from the work of Morten Ryhl-Svendsen and the Indoor Air Pollution Working Group organised by the National Museum of Denmark in a series of international conferences is also to be found on http://hjem.get2net.dk/ryhl/iap.htm
14. Shepilova p.5.
15. Thomson (1988) pp.133-135.
16. Walsh gives specific recommendations on equipment; see also Duchein (1988) pp.110-11; Thomson (1965).
17. See the notes by WH Langwell in *JSA* 1(1955-59), pp.291-3; and 2 (1960-64), pp.166, 221-222.
18. BSI *Guide* p.29.
19. BSI *Guide* p.19. See also Webb and Barton (2002). On the measurement of airtightness and air exchange rates see *Guidelines on pollution control in museum buildings*, 2000, p.13, cited in the Bibliography under Museums Association.
20. Faber and Kell p.349; McIntyre p.279.
21. BSI Guide ch.5.

Chapter 8: Conversion of Existing Buildings

1. Among works cited in the Bibliography, those by Duchein, Nicol and Salisbury are particularly relevant, as well as the papers under the citation *Archive buildings and the conservation of archival material*, pp. 218-225, 262-264. Salisbury p.9 includes an assessment method.
2. Haymond p.14.
3. Haymond p.13.
4. This list is informed by Bordass p.54.

BIBLIOGRAPHY

Note: This select bibliography covers references cited in the text, and also works (mainly published since 1993) that have been taken into account in the writing of this volume. Some earlier publications are noted in the bibliography in Archive buildings in the United Kingdom 1977-1992. *Published references to buildings featured as case studies in the present volume are given separately within the case studies and are generally not repeated here unless of wider significance.*

Adelstein, PZ, 'The why, how, what and where of image permanence standards', in *JSA* 20 no 1 (1999) pp.41-47.

Aleppo, M, 'Fumigation?' in *Archives* 82 (October 1989) pp.74-77.

Allard, F (ed), *Natural ventilation in buildings: a design handbook* (1998).

Allsopp, B, *The modern theory of architecture* (1984).

American Library Association:
   Building blocks for planning functional library space (Lanham MD and London, 2001).
   see also Leighton

Anderson, P, 'Thomas Thomson House – five years on', in *Atlanti* 11 no 2 (2001) pp.158-167.

Anderson, P, 'Recent developments in fire suppression', in *Atlanti* 12 no.1 (2002) pp.97-101.

Archive buildings and the conservation of archival material [proceedings of an expert meeting held in Vienna, 1985] in *Mitteilungen des Österreichischen Staatsarchivs*, 30 (1986) pp.197-289.

Atlanti: The journal of the Archive Centre for Professional and Technical Problems, Maribor, Slovenia, 1991- . A number of citations appear below under names of the individual authors.

Australian Archives, Standards Australia and Standards New Zealand, *Guidelines for mobile shelving for archives, libraries and museums* (1997).

Ballantyne, D, 'Conservation areas in the new building of the National Archives in Canada', in *Janus*, 1995.2 p.94.

Bell, L:
   'The archivist and his accommodation', in *Archivaria* 8 (1979) pp.83-90.
   (and Faye, B) *La conception des bâtiments d'archives en pays tropical* (Unesco, Paris, 1979).

Berge, B (transl. F Henley), *The ecology of building materials* (Oxford, 2001).

Bond, D and Vaid, A, *Archive education services* (Society of Archivists Best Practice Guidelines 5, 1998), Appendix 3: 'Designing, furnishing and equipping an archive education room'.

Bordass, B (ed. M Cassar), *Museum collections in industrial buildings. A selection and adaptation guide* (Museums & Galleries Commission, 1996).

Bordass, B: *see also* Museums Association.

BRECSU [Building Research Energy Conservation Support Unit]
   Among many advisory publications:
   Selecting air-conditioning systems: a guide for building clients and their advisers (Good practice guide 71, 1993, reprinted 1997).
   Briefing the design team for energy efficiency in new buildings (Good practice guide 74, 1996).
   Aspects of energy management (General information report 12, 1996).

British Standards Institution [BSI]:
   [Note: British Standards are subject to periodic review. The current version should always be the one used for reference]
   BS 1153 *Recommendations for processing and storage of silver-gelatine-type microfilm*
   BS 3621 *Thief resistant lock assemblies. Key egress.*
   BS 4783 *Storage, transportation and maintenance of media for use in data processing and information storage* (in several parts).
   BS 5454 *Recommendations for the storage and exhibition of archival documents* (and other Standards to which this refers).
   [BSI Guide] *Archival documents: guide to the interpretation of BS 5454:2000* by C Kitching, H Edgar and I Milford (DISC PD0024, 2001).
   BS 5544 *Specification for anti-bandit glazing ...*
   BS 5979 *Code of practice for remote centres receiving signals from security systems.*
   BS 6262 *Glazing for buildings* (in several parts).
   BS 7273 *Code of practice for the operation of fire protection measures* (in several parts.)
   BS 8220 *Guide for security of buildings against crime* (in several parts).

Buchmann, W:
   'Der Neubau für das Bundesarchiv in Koblenz', in *Archivum* 31 (1986) pp.27-36.
   'Planning an archive building: the cooperation between architect and archivist', in *Archive buildings and the conservation of archival material* (Mitteilungen des Österreichischen Staatsarchivs 39 (Vienna 1986) pp.202-217).

Burke, RB and Adeloye, S, *A manual of basic museum security* (ICOM/ICMS, 1986).

Carassi, M and Massabo Ricci, I, 'Adapting an ancient archives building in Turin', in *Atlanti* 1 (1991) p.25.

Carver, M, 'Lighting design and energy efficiency in museums and galleries', in Cassar, ed (1994) pp.73-96.

Cassar, M:
(ed), *Museums environment energy* (Museums and Galleries Commission and HMSO,1994). Includes management guidelines on energy efficiency.
Environmental management: Guidelines for museums and galleries (1995).
(ed.), *Delivering a successful museum building* (Royal Armouries Museum, 1999).
see also Museums Association.

Centre for Sustainable Heritage [University College London], *Climate change and the historic environment* (2005).

Centro de Información Documental de Archivos [Madrid]: *Boletín*, a periodical bibliography including a section on archive buildings. *See also* www.mcu.es/index.jsp and then link to Centros de Documentación.

Chartered Institute of Building (CIOB), *The procurement and management of construction* (www.ciob.org.uk).

Chartered Institute of Building Services Engineers *see* CIBSE

Child, RE, 'Insect pests in archives: detection, monitoring and control', in *JSA* 20 no 2 (1999) pp.141-148.

Childs, RJ, *Health and Safety. A guide to good health and safety practice in the record office* (Society of Archivists Best Practice Guideline 3, 1996).

Chitty, R and Fraser-Mitchell, J, *Fire safety engineering: a reference guide* (BRE, 2003).

Christoffersen, L, *ZEPHYR: Passive climate controlled repositories: storage facilities for museum, archive and library purposes* (B&K, Virum, Denmark, 1995).

CIBSE (Chartered Institute of Building Services Engineers):
Guide to lighting in museums (1993).
Fire engineering (CIBSE Guide E, 6th edn, 1997).

CILIP *see* Library Association

Collis, IP, 'The ideal layout of a local record repository', in *Archives*, 1 nos 6 and 7 (1951-1952).

Cox, H, 'The state of environmental monitoring in museums, libraries and archives', in NPO e-Journal, October 2004 (www.bl.uk/services/npo/journal/2/environment.html).

Crosby, J, 'Fire precautions in archive repositories in the UK', in *Atlanti* 2 (1993) pp.38-44.

DCMS [Department for Culture, Media and Sport]:
Better public buildings: a proud legacy for the future (2000).
People and places: social inclusion policy for the built and historic environment (2002).

DETR [Department for the Environment, Transport and the Regions]:
Rethinking construction (1998).
Climate change: draft UK programme (2000).

den Teuling, A
(trans. E Ponwels) *Requirements for the building and equipment of repositories and the conversion or refurbishment or adaptation of buildings or parts of buildings for repositories* (Assen, NL, 4th edn 1994).
'Environmental conditions for the storage of archives', in *Janus* 1996.2 pp.110-118.

Department for Trade and Industry, *see* DTI

Department for Culture, Media and Sport, *see* DCMS

Department for the Environment, Transport and the Regions, *see* DETR

Dewe, M (ed), *Library buildings: preparation for planning* (IFLA publications no 48, 1989).

DTI [Department for Trade and Industry]:
Fire fighting. Halon phase out; Advice on alternatives and guidelines for users (Undated booklet, c.1994).

Duchein, M:
Archive buildings and equipment (ICA handbooks series, vol. 6, 2nd revised and enlarged edn, ed P Walne, transl. D Thomas, 1988).
'Protection of archives against water damage', in *Atlanti* 3 (1993).

Dunn, FI, *Security* (Society of Archivists Best Practice Guideline 2, 1994).

Edgar, H *see* BSI.

Feather, J and Eden, P, *National Preservation Policy: Policies and practices in archives and record offices* (British Library, 1997).

Fire Protection Association [FPA]. Data sheets, including *The secure building envelope* (Data sheet 14).

Follette, L, 'Help. We can't breathe in here! The effects of limited air circulation within mobile shelving units', in *Records Management Quarterly*, April 1991.

France, Direction des Archives de :
Manuel d'archivistique (1970).
'La conservation préventive des documents graphiques: L'étude Lambert commandée par la Direction des archives de France', in *Janus* 1997.2.
Ermisse, G., Marguin Hamon, E and Saïe Belaïsch, F, *Bâtiments d'archives 1986-2003* (Paris, 2004).

Giovannini, A, 'Architecture and preservation: fighting the same battle', in *International Preservation Management*, 22-23 (Aug-Dec 2000) pp. 5-18.

Gondos, V jr, 'Archival buildings: programming and planning', in *American Archivist* 27 no 4 (1964) pp.467-583.

[Great Lakes Chemical Corporation], Understanding the thermal decomposition of FM200® and the effect on people and equipment (1997) [*see* www.

el.greatlakes.com/wfp/common/jsp/index.jsp]

Hanus, J, 'Environmental degradation and protection of archival documents', in *Atlanti* 12 no 1 (2002) pp.28-41.

Harrison, D (ed), *Library buildings in the United Kingdom 1990-1994* (1995).

Haymond, J., 'Adaptive reuse of old buildings for archives', in *American Archivist*, 45 no 1 (1982) pp.11-18.

Health and Safety Executive, *The Work at Height Regulations 2005. A brief guide* (www.hse.gov.uk/pubns/indg401.pdf

Hofenk de Graaff, JH et al., 'The effect of alkaline boxes and file folders on the accelerated ageing of paper by air pollution', in *Janus* 1996.2 pp.102-109.

Horsman, P, 'Smart archival buildings: ICT in archives', in *Atlanti* 8 (1998), pp.73-81.

International Council on Archives [ICA]:
Bibliography on archive buildings and equipment [among the publications of the former committee on archive buildings and equipment (CBTE) on the ICA website, www.ica.org and then link to 'download center'. Includes a number of case studies].
Memory of the World at Risk: Archives destroyed, archives reconstituted. (*Archivum* XLII, 1996). Includes bibliography on disaster control.
Guidelines on disaster prevention and control in archives (ICA Studies 11, 1997). Includes practical guidance on fixtures and fittings for good management to avoid disasters.
see also Duchein.

International Federation of Library Associations [IFLA]:
IFLA principles for the care and handling of library materials, (International Preservation Issues 1, 1998, comp. EP Adcock).

International Organisation for Standardisation (ISO) :
ISO 11799 Information and documentation – Document storage requirements.
ISO 14001 :2004 Environmental management systems. Requirements with guidance for use.

Jost, HP et al, 'Constructions écologiques de bâtiments d'archives', in *Janus* 1996.2 pp.97-101.

Keene, JA and Roper, M, *Planning, equipping and staffing a document reprographic service* (Unesco RAMP study, Paris 1984, PGI-84/WS/8).

Kennett, S, 'Soaking up the atmosphere' [Jersey Archive], in *Building Services Journal*, August 2001 pp.50-52.

Kidd, S, *Fire risk management in historic buildings* (Historic Scotland, Technical Conservation Research and Education Division, Technical Advice Note 22 (2001). Includes a case study : 'The National Library of Scotland: risk improvement in a major national institution'.

Kitching, C:
Archive buildings in the United Kingdom 1977-

1992 (1993).
Archives. The very essence of our heritage (Chichester, 1996).
'BS 5454:2000, the evolution of a standard', in *JSA* 21 no 2 (2000) pp. 159-167.
'Preservation in new buildings', in *LIBER Quarterly*, 10 no 2 (2000) pp.376-386.
'BS5454:2000, the implications for libraries', in *NPO Journal* 9 (October 2001) pp.275-277.
see also British Standards Institution.

Klasinc, PP
'Negative working exeriences in new or adapted archival buildings', in *Atlanti* 11 no 2 (2001) pp.121-129.
'The protection of archival records from environmental effects', in *Atlanti* 12 no 1 (2002) pp.22-27.

Konya, A, *Libraries, a briefing and design guide* (1986).

Lafrenière, Carole, 'Conservation areas in the new building of the National Archives of Canada', in *Association of Commonwealth Archivists and Records Managers Newsletter* 18 (Dec 1996) p.18.

Leighton, PD and Weber, DC, *Planning academic and research library buildings* (3rd edn, American Library Association, Chicago and London 1999).

Library Association [now CILIP]:
'Fire rekindles debate', in *Record* 96 no 9 (September 1994) p.67.

Ling, T, *Solid, safe, secure: building archives repositories in Australia* (National Archives of Australia [1998], ISBN 0 642 34403 5.

MacKenzie, G:
'Layout and equipment in conservation areas', in *Janus* 1995.2 p.101.
(and Ramsay, L) 'An integrated approach to preservation: the new Scottish Record Office building in Edinburgh', in *La conservation: une science en évolution* (Actes des troisièmes journées internationales d'études de l'ARSAG, Paris 1997).

McCormick-Goodhart, MH, 'The allowable temperature and relative humidity range for the safe use and storage of photographic materials', in *JSA* 17 no 1 (1996) pp.7-21.

Matthews, G and Eden, P, *Disaster management in British libraries ...* (British Library: Library and Information Research Report 109, 1996).

Mead, A, 'Architectural archive reveals a passion for history', in *Architects' Journal*, 29 June 1994 pp.17-19.

Milford, I *see* BSI.

MLA (Museums, Libraries and Archives Council) www.mla.gov.uk :
Disability Portfolio Guidelines.

Museums Association, *Guidelines on pollution control in museum buildings* (Museums Association 2000, distributed with *Museum Practice* no 15, November 2000). Jointly authored by N Blades, T Oreszczyn, B Bordass and M Cassar.

Neirinck, D :
'L'aménagement des bâtiments anciens en bâtiments d'archives en France', in *Atlanti* 1 (1991) p.42.
'La protection contre l'incendie dans les bâtiments d'archives', in *Atlanti* 2 (1993) pp.52-55.
'La sécurité des documents: lutte contre le vol et les actes de vandalisme', in *Atlanti* 3 (1993) pp.33-37.
(and Benoit, G) 'L'évolution de la conception des bâtiments d'archives', in *La conservation: une science en évolution: bilans et perspectives.* (ARSAG, Paris, 1997).
Nicol, A, 'Archival buildings: purpose-built or converted', in Norton pp.19-22.
Norton, A (ed.), *Archives in '86* (INLOGOV, Birmingham, 1986).
Padfield, T:
'Condensation in the walls of humidified buildings' (1997) (*www.natmus.dk/cons/tp/condens/*).
The role of absorbent building materials in moderating changes of relative humidity (Technical University of Denmark, Dept of Structural Engineering and Materials, reports series R no 54 (1999): www.bkm.dtu.dk).
Pearson, A, 'Totally absorbing' [Jersey Archive], in *Building*, August 1999 pp.44-45.
Pearson, BP, *An inquiry into the fire at the Norwich Central Library on the 1st August 1994* (Norwich 1995).
Pinniger, D, *Pest management in museums, archives and historic houses* (2001).
Public Services Quality Group [PSQG] *see* website www.ncaonline.org.uk/psqg/access
PULMAN [Public Libraries Mobilising Advanced Networks]: *The PULMAN Guidelines*, 2nd edn 2003 (*see* www.pulmanweb.org).
Ratcliffe, FW, 'Preparing for the planning and design of a library building', in Dewe pp.13-28.
Reading, A, 'Air-conditioning, energy efficiency and environmental control; can all three co-exist?' in Cassar, ed (1994) pp.39-46.
Robinson, D, 'Surrey History Centre: the experience of lottery application', in *JSA* 18 no 2 (1997) pp.151-163.
Rombouts, W, 'Quelques problèmes concernant la construction des bâtiments d'archives et des matériaux utilisés en Europe', in *Janus* 1996.2 pp.87-96.
Roper, M, *Planning, equipping and staffing an archival preservation and conservation service* (Unesco RAMP study, Paris 1989, PGI-89/WS/4).
Rowoldt, S, 'The greening of archive buildings. Natural air-conditioning in the Southern African context', in *Janus* 1993.2 p.36.
Salisbury, F, *Briefing your architect* (2nd edn, Oxford, 1998).

Sannwald, WW, *Checklist of library building design considerations* (4th edn, ALA, Chicago and London, 2001).
Shepilova, IG, *Main principles of fire protection in libraries and archives* (Unesco RAMP study, Paris 1992, PGI-92/WS/14).
Shields, TJ and Silcock, WH, *Buildings and fire* (1987).
Simonet, JE, 'Protection against theft and burglary in archive buildings' (typescript of a paper given at the ICA committee on archive buildings and equipment, Vienna 1990, subsequently printed in French in *Janus*, 1992.1, pp.101-105).
Smith, DP, 'Water mist fire suppression systems', in *Fire Safety Engineering* 2 no 2 (1995) pp.10-15.
Smith, PF, *Architecture in a climate of change: a guide to sustainable design* (Oxford, 2001).
Stonehouse, R and Stromberg, G, *The architecture of the British Library at St Pancras* (2004).
Swartzburg, SG and Bussey, H (with F Garretson), *Libraries and archives: design and renovation with a preservation perspective* (Lanham MD, 1998). A bibliography with commentary.
Thomas, DL, 'Archive buildings: international comparisons', in *JSA* 9 (1988) pp.38-44.
Thomason, G, 'Stabilisation of relative humidity in exhibition cases: hygrometric half time', in *Studies in Conservation* 22 (1977) pp.85-105.
Thompson, A, *Library buildings of Britain and Europe* (1963).
Thompson, G, *Planning and design of library buildings* (3rd edn, 1989).
Thomson, G:
'Relative humidity variation with temperature in a case containing wood', in *Studies in Conservation* 9 (1964) pp.153-169.
'Air pollution. A review for conservation chemists', in *Studies in Conservation* 10 (1965) pp.145-167.
'Annual exposure to light within museums', in *Studies in Conservation* 12 (1967) pp.26-35.
The museum environment (2nd edn,1986).
Walch, T, *Archives & manuscripts: security* (Society of American Archivists basic manuals series, Chicago 1977 revised 1980).
Webb, BC and Barton, R., *Airtightness in commercial buildings* (BRE, 2002).
Williams, D, 'Defining an archive: the Jersey experience' in *JSA* 22 no 2 (2001) pp125-138.
Woods, C:
'Designing a conservation room an example from Dorset', in *JSA* 13 no 2 (1992) pp.132-135.
'Meeting the Montreal Protocol: alternative fire suppression systems for archives', in *JSA* 23 no 2 (2002) pp.179-186.
Young, R, 'Gaseous fire extinguishing agents as halon 1301 alternatives', in *Fire prevention* 277 (March 1995).

SYNOPSIS OF SUBJECTS IN PART ONE

*Note: Subjects are grouped thematically, and not always alphabetically, under fourteen main headings indicated by **bold type**. Because archive storage areas are mentioned in every chapter they are not included here. Similarly, the Case Studies in Part Two each cover most of the main headings below, and are therefore not included in the synopsis but should be consulted individually.*

Archive buildings (see also Structure)
character, ch 1
conversion/purpose building, ch 8; 6, 32, 33, 47, 58, 142
    types of building converted, 70
design/aesthetic considerations, 10-12, 14, 24,29, 40-1
expansion space, 7, 25, 40, 68
funding, 1, 5, 7, 9, 11
    plural sources, 2
    role of HLF, 1, 11
out-stores, 6

Archives and archive services
infrastructure, statutes and regulations, 2, 5, 10, 20, 23, 31
issues affecting particular media:
    cellulose nitrate, 19,52
    new media [film, sound etc], 13, 14, 16, 18, 24, 42, 50, 59, 61
nature and importance of archives, ch 1; 14
partnership with other services, 1, 2
public access, 2, 3, 13, 14, 48-9, 50
    by disabled people, 2, 23
rate of accumulation of archives, 5
weight of archives, 34

Environment, indoor, ch 7 (see also Structure, high thermal inertia)
air-conditioning, ch 7; 3, 36-8
air circulation, ch 7;16, 20, 21
air quality/pollution, 3, 62, 64
    filtration and washing, 58, 59, 63, 64
    ventilation, 3, 20, 36, 59
control of temperature and relative humidity, ch 7; 3, 13, 14, 15, 18, 23, 36-8, 42, 44
    acclimatisation, 16, 18, 19, 33
lighting, 23, 24
natural climatisation, 3, 36-7, 44, 59, 62, 63

Environment, outdoor (see also Structure, orientation)
weather, protection against, 10, 28, 34-5, 42, 43, 45, 62-3;

Environmental concerns
climate change, 3, 28, 35, 37, 62
energy consumption, 9, 22, 38-40, 58, 60, 62, 65, 74
environmental impact of buildings, 27, 29-30, 39, 40
fire-fighting and, 55

Equipment and fittings, ch 2
air-conditioning equipment, ch 7
    BMS, 62
    maintenance of, 64
alarms, see Hazards, fire; Security
art, commissioned works of, 1, 45-6
blinds, 44, 65
carpets, 24, 42, 45
CCTV, 23, 49
computers, digitisation etc, 2, 7, 9, 13, 16, 21, 23, 24, 44, 48
electrical, 22, 53
electrostatic dust-precipitators, 60
exhibition display cases, 23, 24
fans, 59-60, 63
fire extingishers, 56
for conservation, 20-21,39
for lecture rooms, 25
for meeting rooms, 25
humidifiers/dehumidifiers, 36, 59, 64
lighting, 65-6
    emergency lighting, 20
lockers, 23, 50
microfilm readers, 24, 44, 51
plant, see Functions
roller shutters, 45
security lighting, 49
shelving, 34, 77
    and fire prevention, 19, 54
    height, 20
    mezzanine, 42
    mobile, 19-20, 34, 42-3, 63
    wooden, 19
tables/desks and chairs, 23, 24, 39, 65
telephones, 16, 20
torches, 20
trolleys, 16, 42
water services, 22-3, 42, 68

Fire, see Hazards

Functions in an archive building
in general, ch 2; 6, 11, 141
    importance of flexibility, 13, 25, 42, 68
checklist, 13-16
    flow diagram, 17
particular functions, 15ff
    accessioning/reception, 16
    conservation, 14, 20-21, 39, 42, 44, 53, 65, 66
    computer rooms, 21
    education/lecture rooms, 25

exhibition, 23
interview room, 24
isolation, 16
    fumigation, 16
loading bay, 15-16, 49
on-line access, 2, 24
plant, 14, 20, 22, 45, 53
public areas, 14, 23-5, 42, 44, 48, 49, 51, 65
reprographics, 14, 21, 45
safe room 19, 48
sorting, 16
staff offices and facilities, 14, 21-2, 42
storage space, general, 21, 25
viewing/listening facilities, 24
relationships between, ch 2
segregation of, ch 2

Hazards
in general, 10, 14, 27
    risk management, 28, 32, 48, 52-3
associated with site, ch 5
particular hazards:
    aircraft, 28
    birds, 30
    condensation, 38, 42, 43, 44, 54
    contaminated land, 27, 29
    dust, 10, 27-8, 37, 42, 44, 63, 64
    earthquake, 28
    explosion, 27-8, 34
    fire, ch 6; 3, 10, 13, 14, 22, 27-8, 30, 31, 47, 142
        alarms, 22, 50, 53, 68
        compartments, 33
        detection, 2, 32
        extinction, 32, 53ff
        gas, 2, 33, 42, 52, 55-6
        water, 2, 33, 52, 54-5
        resistance, 31ff, 41ff, 45, 68
    light, 20, 44, 65-6
    lightning, 34, 44, 66
    mould, 10, 16, 58, 63
    noise/soundproofing, 13, 15, 24, 27, 42
    pests, 10, 16, 30, 42, 44, 58, 64
    pollutants, 10, 27-8, 41, 44, 62-3
    smoke, 32
    terrorism, 34
    theft, 10, 14, 47-51
    vandalism, 10, 27-8, 47-9
    water/flood, 3, 10, 14, 20, 22, 27, 28, 34ff
        alarms, 22
        drainage, 14, 22, 35, 42, 68
        waterproofing, 21, 22, 34

Health and safety
in general, 14-15, 41, 64, 68
in particular:
    humidifier fever, 64
    legionnaire's disease, 64
    sick building syndrome, 64

Materials, ch 4; 3, 9, 24, 58

Planning, ch 1
brief, 8, 10, 11, 13, 26
costs, 8, 9, 11, 12, 39
    Whole Life Costing, 9, 60
    value engineering, 9
period of occupancy, 6, 7
procurement, 9
risk management, see Hazards
role of architect, 7, 8, 9, 10-12, 67
shared premises, 73
tendering, 7, 8
time scale, 7, 8

Security, ch 5; 13, 14, 15, 19, 23, 30, 33ff, 44, 45, 56, 142
alarms, 15, 23, 47-50
locks, 50

Site, ch 3; 7-9, 13, 39, 67, 72, 141
archaeology, 29
landscaping, 30, 34, 49

Structure, ch 4; 141
air-tightness, 38, 55, 56, 64, 72
    pressure-resistance, 55
basements, 35, 54, 69
compartments, 33, 68-9
drying out, 8, 20, 35
fire resistance, see Hazards, fire
floor-loading, 19, 20, 24, 68
foundations, 27, 29, 34, 68
high thermal inertia, 9, 36ff, 40
maintenance, 9, 39, 43, 68
of converted buildings, ch 8; 10, 15, 34, 43, 45, 49, 58
orientation, 20, 28, 44, 58, 62, 67, 72
particular features:
    air vents, 33, 36, 44
    ceilings, 31, 32, 42, 69
        suspended, 43
    chimneys, 33, 69
    columns, 16, 43, 51, 69
    corridors, 15, 22, 40
    doors, 15, 31, 32, 33, 45, 49, 50, 57
    drainpipes, 34
    Faraday cage, 18
    fire escapes, 49, 52, 57
    floors, 31, 42-3, 68
        coverings, 15, 42
    lifts, 16, 32, 50-1, 68
    perimeter, 40, 49, 51
    roofs, 34, 43, 68
        flat, 43
    walls, 13, 15, 21, 24, 31, 36, 41ff, 69
    partitions, 13, 42
    windows, 32, 33, 34, 44, 68
        baffles, 44
    skylight, 43, 51
shape, 13, 39ff, 51, 68, 72
underground storage, 28, 37